ENERGY THROUGH TIME

Teacher's Guide

Joe Scott and Denis Shemilt

Oxford University Press 1986

The Schools History Project 13–16

The Schools History Project 13–16 was formerly the Schools Council History Project. It was first set up in 1972 at the University of Leeds, to reconsider the objectives of teaching history in the middle secondary years and to produce materials for a new course. GCE and CSE examinations based on this course were first set in 1976. By 1985 about 40,000 candidates entered for these examinations. From 1988 GCSE examinations will be set by all the Examining Groups on syllabuses based on the Project course.

The Project is at present based at the Centre for History Education, Trinity and All Saints College, Brownberrie Lane, Horsforth, Leeds LS18 5HD. Its Director is Ian Dawson, from whom further information may be obtained. See page 53 for a list of books and articles about the Project. Information about examination syllabuses and regulations may be obtained from the examination boards.

Oxford University Press, Walton Street, Oxford OX2 6DP

Oxford New York Toronto
Delhi Bombay Calcutta Madras Karachi
Petaling Jaya Singapore Hong Kong Tokyo
Nairobi Dar es Salaam Cape Town
Melbourne Auckland

and associated companies in
Beirut Berlin Ibadan Nicosia

Oxford is a trade mark of Oxford University Press

© Oxford University Press 1986

ISBN 0 19 913323 9

Typesetting by: Qualitext Typesetting.

Illustrations by: Sharp Image Graphic Design, Chris Knight Graphic Design

Printed in Great Britain

Contents

1: Aims and objectives

The main aim of the Schools History Project is to enhance pupils' grasp of those historical concepts and mastery of those historical skills which adolescents growing up in the world of today will find valuable. The examination course has four main parts, a Study in Development, an Enquiry in Depth, a Modern World Study, and a study of 'History Around Us'. Each of these is designed with special reference to particular skills and concepts, though they have many common objectives, such as a common insistence on the importance of the evaluation of evidence. 'Energy through Time' is one of the alternative Studies in Development.

1: The aims of the studies in development

The main aim is to improve pupils' ideas of development, change, continuity and causation.

Many children of 14 have naive ideas of historical change as a series of disconnected episodes, or of development as an inevitable 'march of progress'. Many have a vague and imprecise chronological 'map' of the past, ornamented by a jumble of events arranged in no very clear perspective. The studies in development provide materials with which students may improve their perspective and develop a more sophisticated grasp of the processes and nature of historical change.

A secondary aim, shared with all other parts of the Project course, is to reinforce the idea that history is an enquiry into evidence rather than a series of established truths, and to develop skills in handling various forms of historical evidence.

These aims might be served equally by any and every 'Study in Development', and are thus independent of the content of the course. Knowledge of the content, though needed to give substance to the course, is not a major aim in itself.

2: Why 'Energy through Time'?

There are three reasons why 'Energy through Time' was chosen as the second 'Study in Development', alternative to 'Medicine Through Time'. The first is that, like medicine, energy is a topic of key importance in all periods of history. Like medicine it demonstrates continuities and provides examples of rapid and gradual change. Like medicine it provides opportunities to show how general political, social and intellectual changes, such as the coming of the first literate societies or of the industrial revolution, had particular effects in one specific field.

A second reason for the choice of energy is its relevance in today's world. Problems of energy supply and conservation and problems of the effects of energy use, such as pollution, are parts of everyday experience as well as of political debate. This makes energy a useful topic to reinforce the historian's message that the present is the product of the past and to demonstrate that history can help towards political understanding.

A third reason for the choice of energy is that it may be used to encourage technological and economic literacy, and to show pupils that history is not a member of only one of CP Snow's 'Two Cultures', but firmly bridges the artificial divide between them.

3: Starting positions – what pupils need to bring to the course

A: **General skills and concepts**

1: A moderate level of literacy is expected: that of a pupil likely to attain GCSE grade G at age 16. The book has been structured to make the literacy demands as low as possible, but the levels needed vary, particularly in the sources, and teachers should be selective. The book is not a text-book to be worked through slavishly or a reading book to be swallowed whole.

2: A moderate level of numeracy including the ability to read simple line graphs, block graphs and pie charts.

3: The ability to use maps and some outline knowledge of the world map and of the maps of Britain and Europe.

4: A familiarity at a *simple* level with everyday modern technologies. For example the knowledge that many domestic machines are powered by electricity, which is made in power stations, or that motor vehicles use petrol which is an oil product coming from wells.

5: A *general* grasp of some scientific principles: such as knowledge that fossils are the remains of long dead living matter, or that the atmosphere has pressure which can squash things, or that all matter is made up of atoms.

B: **Historical skills and concepts**

1: Some grasp of the following ideas;
a) History is an enquiry based on the evaluation of evidence, and not a series of revealed truths.
b) History is a rational study in which cause and motive can be understood, and not a series of random events.
c) The idea of empathy – that one important way to make sense of the actions of people in the past is to try to 'see things through their eyes.'

2: Some chronological sense of events changing and developing. The ability to use terms like 'Prehistoric' 'Ancient Times' 'the Middle Ages', BC and AD. Familiarity with the idea of time charts.

3: The knowledge that the agricultural (or neolithic) revolution, the urban revolution and the industrial revolution are important episodes in human history.

| 4: Enabling concepts – needed as the course progresses | Some skills or concepts which are not themselves objectives of the course are necessary before certain sources can be used effectively, or the significance of certain events understood. Teachers may wish at the appropriate point to organise work specifically designed to establish these 'enabling concepts'. For example some understanding of the idea of the investment of capital is important in energy history from the | partnership of Boulton and Watt to the modern oil multinationals. In the field of technology, some idea of the distinction between alternating and direct current is needed before the history of the transmission of electric power can be grasped. References are made to such concepts at the points in the Teachers' Book where they may be useful. |

5: Finishing lines – intended learning outcomes

A: Target objectives

At the end of their study of 'Energy through Time' pupils should have:

1: An overview of the main *changes and trends* in man's use of energy. This can be broken down into:
a) familiarity with the following lines of development;
i) a series of 'prime movers': animal power, water-power, wind-power, steam engines, internal combustion engines.
ii) a series of fuels: wood, charcoal, coal, oil, uranium.
iii) a series of methods of transporting fuel, from pack animals to oil tankers.
iv) a rapidly expanding demand for energy from the 16th to the late 20th century.
b) awareness of how energy technologies have spread from one region to another, particularly in the Middle Ages and in the 19th century.
c) awareness of the impact of the 'high energy' civilisation of the 20th century on the developing world.

2: An understanding of how the following *turning points* in the history of energy and in general history are linked together:

b) there have been periods of stagnation or decline.

4: An appreciation that the history of energy includes some *continuities* and some *discontinuities*. For instance some problems like fuel shortages have been present at many periods, while in the 19th century a quite new realisation emerged that world supplies of fossil fuels are limited in amount

5: Some understanding of the *causes of change* in the history of energy, including:
a) The role played by long term factors which have encouraged or inhibited change at different times, such as transport, science and war.
b) The web of interrelation between the various factors that brought about particular developments at particular times, such as the greatly increased use of water power in the Middle Ages; the development of the steam engine in the 18th century.
c) The role of individuals in causing or preventing change, eg Newcomen, Watt, Boulton, Edison.
d) The role of organised groups in causing or preventing change, e.g. Lords of Manors in the Middle Ages, conservation pressure groups at various periods.
e) Ability to distinguish between long-term and

Changes in society	Turning points in energy use
a) The coming of agriculture	a) Pottery, harnessing animals
b) The coming of organised civilisation	b) Great increase in energy needs
c) The increased wealth and power of West Europeans 1500–1800	c) Reliance on fossil fuels begins in 17th century Britain. The coming of the steam engine with its capacity to turn heat into mechanical power.
d) The coming of exact science after the Renaissance	d) The coming of science-based energy technologies in the 19th and 20th centuries, especially electricity, with its capacity to transmit energy over a distance.
e) The development of technologically advanced societies in the 19th and 20th centuries.	e) Very greatly increased demand for the production and transmission of energy. A world market in energy.

3: Some understanding of the *varying pace of change* in the history of energy. Pupils should have refined the naive ideas about progress with which they are likely to have started the course, and should be able to discuss whether in the history of energy:
a) there has been steady improvement in some respects, or in a general sense.

short-term causes, and to see that some factors were more important than others in a given context.
f) Ability to distinguish between immediate and long term consequences, and to see that some consequences were unexpected or unintended.

2: Planning the Course

1: How long and when?

The work on the Study in Development is about a quarter of the entire SHP 14–16 course, and should take up about 1½ terms. Some teachers have found that with its prehistoric start and its broad chronological sweep it is a useful introduction to the SHP course. Others argue that since it is the only part of the course which is assessed entirely in the written papers, it is best to study it in year 5.

2: Schemes of work

Scheme 1

The pupils' book is designed round this approach which was found to be effective by many teachers with the Medicine development study.

Stage 1: Introduction to persuade pupils of the interest and importance of the topic.

Stage 2: Rapid narrative overview. The main aim is to establish a framework or 'story-line' sufficiently firm to support ideas and information gained in Stages 3 and 4. The amount of detail included and the speed of movement will vary with the ability of the pupils. So will the time taken, but it is suggested that a period of 5–6 weeks might be a reasonable one.

Stage 3: Study of selected factors. All pupils should study at least two factors, and the more able all five of those treated in the pupils' book and/or others. As well as consolidating overview this is designed to encourage thinking in causal terms by the artificial device of isolating single factors.

Stage 4: Study of historiographic problems using material from the history of energy. The 'Energy through Time' course is a study in development and not a history of energy. The main aim is to refine the pupils' assumptions about historical development in ways that transfer to further study of history and to adult life. All pupils should consider all five problems raised, but at varying levels.

Scheme 2

Just as a scheme of work of the type outlined above has been used with the chronologically arranged 'Medicine through Time' materials, so a scheme which spent longer on a chronological treatment of the narrative would be possible using 'Energy through Time'.

Stage 1: Introduction as in Scheme 1

Stage 2: Identification (by discussion of the contemporary energy scene) of key factors (Transport, Shortage, Government, Scientific knowledge) which are to be followed up in Stages 3 and 4.

Stage 3: More leisurely chronological treatment aiming to establish a more solid knowledge of particular periods by the use of the narrative together with additional sources selected from the factors section of the book for each chronological period.

Stage 4: 'Through Time' work on the chosen factors (or others).

Stage 5: Historiographic problems as in Scheme 1.

The dangers of a scheme of this sort are that it may run out of time, and that weaker pupils may be lost in Stage 3. It might be appropriate for a very able group.

3: Internal assessment

Since each stage – narrative, factors, problems – has a different set of objectives, each stage should end with an assessment that can at the same time consolidate and measure progress.

Suggested assessment exercises can be found at the end of the discussion of each of the stages of Scheme 1 on pages 30, 39, and 45

3: Teaching the course

1: Teaching style and pupil progress

The following suggestions are based on the experience of the Project during the first ten years of its operation.

A: **Coherence and variety in teaching**

No teaching methods appear to be good or bad in themselves, but excessive reliance on a narrow range of methods is clearly less effective than use of a variety. Variety must not, however, endanger coherence. Many teachers have experience of methods and exercises successful in other contexts that nevertheless proved disastrous in their own classrooms, either because they themselves lacked the skill needed, or, more often, because their pupils were unfamiliar with the material or the methods of thinking involved. Variety is important but congruence of elements and materials is more important still. As established Project teachers testify, pupils must be habituated to certain ways of working in History – to thinking instead of copying and memorizing, to working in pairs or groups as well as by themselves, and to thinking about possibilities instead of 'right answers'. These things can take time.

Two ways in which teaching can be made varied and active are
i) use of pair and group work
ii) use of oral, pictorial and diagrammatic methods of recording and analysing historical material. Drama, simulations, cartoon strips and models are all useful tasks for group work, especially if groups include less literate pupils. History is in many ways essentially a literary

subject, but this need not preclude a greater emphasis on non-literary modes of representation than has traditionally been the case. Even though such methods set for the teacher more problems of preparation and even of classroom control than traditional methods, they have great value in bringing pupils face to face with historical problems about which they can think for themselves.

The Study in Development also offers scope for quantitative work of many kinds. History is a quantitative subject involving generalisations based on statistics, some of them often questionable. Energy through Time offers many opportunities for numerical work, from simple counting to complex statistics. It demands mathematical reasoning about human affairs, as in discussions of the last 150 years about the depletion of fossil fuel reserves. It leads on to a consideration of the assumptions that lie behind the statistics, and of what can legitimately be asserted about human affairs on their basis. Teaching methods should take advantage of these opportunities.

B: The elimination of 'clutter'

Recent HMI and DES documents stress the need to purge the secondary curriculum of 'clutter'. Research evidence also suggests that pupils, and particularly the less able ones, are swamped by information. Public examinations clearly show that Project candidates able to display conceptual understanding and historical skills, or to memorise facts accurately, frequently fail to acquire an organised and usable 'map' of syllabus content based on a coherent conception of the whole.

History is inevitably an information-rich subject, so it is important
i) to prevent the plethora of data from so clogging pupils' minds that they are unable to see the broad story-line.
ii) to help pupils with the complex task of manipulating and organizing large amounts of data.

This means that pupils should be helped to distinguish between 'durable' and 'disposable' data. Much historical material is of short-term relevance only. It may be useful to add colour, to make a point, to exemplify, to pose a question or to serve as a basis for inference and argument. Once used it may be allowed to fade from memory without loss–it is disposable. Other material, on the other hand must be retained–it is durable. It is vital, for instance, that pupils retain an overview of the 'Energy through Time' story. They cannot begin to consider questions about cause, change and development, nor to construe the historical significance of events, unless they possess some clear overview of the narrative. But this overview must be 'uncluttered'. It need not be detailed, but it must be organised and the items within it must be relevant. Disconnected facts about odd topics are of little value.

It is thus essential;

1: To establish what is to count as a minimum overview. This should be expressed as a story showing change and development through time, not as a list of events.

2: To ensure that pupils record overview information in a way that clearly distinguishes it from 'disposable' notes and exercises. Ideally the overview information should be recorded in a different notebook or file section.

3: To ensure that pupils can reproduce a minimal overview prior to analysis of factors and problems. It may be useful for pupils to reproduce this in a variety of ways—essays, annotated and illustrated time charts, cartoon narratives, or diagrams indicating themes, connections and lines of development.

The following basic overview should be appropriate to the generality of pupils:

c. 500,000 years ago
Humans learned to control fire. This was a great advantage in their struggle for survival, but set them many new technical problems.

c. 10,000 years ago
People in some regions developed farming. This greatly increased their need for energy for industry (pottery) and agriculture. It also supplied them with animal power.

c. 5,500 years ago
People in some regions developed urban societies, bringing new energy needs such as organised war or metal working. It also meant better transport, organised use of human labour, and, after a long delay, water-power.

These changes spread slowly in the Middle East, India, the Mediterranean, China and later in Europe.

c. AD 1500–c. 1875
Europeans used the old energy techniques of water-power, animal power, sailing ships and wood fuel to their limit. This greatly increased the wealth and power of the region. It lead also to other new machines, notably the steam engine which vastly increased human power and also human need for fuel. 'High Energy' society, dependent on a massive use of fossil fuels developed first in Britain and Europe and then spread to other areas.

Since 1875
The high energy using countries developed new forms of energy (electricity, oil and natural gas, nuclear power) and new machines to use them. A world market in energy developed. These new forms of energy transformed everyday life as well as industry, transport, agriculture and war. Since 1945 the explosive demand for energy supplies has led to fears of a world shortage. Energy supply has become an important source of political conflict. High energy use poses many other important problems e.g. pollution. Although the high energy

way of life has spread during this period many poor areas of the world still depend on animal power and wood fuel. The energy poverty of these regions is an important ingredient in the present very great contrast between the rich world and the poor world.

C: Promotion of 'reflective' learning

Pupils do not grasp concepts and acquire skills in history by learning definitions, formulae or algorithms expounded to them by the teacher. They learn by using and refining the concepts and skills they already possess. Pupils invariably have ideas and assumptions about the stories told in history, about how and why things happened in the past, though these ideas and assumptions are rarely articulate. They are pre-conceptual understandings which can only be clarified as the pupils themselves experience difficulty in making sense of the past and come to recognise the limitiations of and the contradictions between their existing ideas. This means that teachers need to do the following;

1: Seek to reconstruct what is going on in pupils' minds. From the fact that certain mistaken or inadequate responses appear to pupils to be sensible and adequate answers to questions, teachers can work out what assumptions pupils are making about the past and about what is involved in historical explanation.

2: Value pupils' ideas and skills, however eccentric or meagre, and seek to reward any development of skill, however slight. Very few pupils will leave school with even an adequate grasp of how and why things happen in human history, but any course that leaves pupils with fewer misconceptions is worthwhile. If a pupil ends the course with little more than a firm conviction that what happens now is somehow related to what happened in the past, or that people have a hand in making history rather than just having it happen to them, then much of value may have been achieved. But it is vital that pupils recognise that their ideas are respected and it is also vital that their progress is measured by how much their ideas develop, rather than by how far they fall short of some unattainable ideal.

3: Encourage pupils to behave reflexively, that is to make of their own ideas objects of reflection, discussion and criticism. Some teachers, for instance have found it profitable to base class discussion on individual or group written work, exploiting differences in conclusions, arguments and explanations, and inviting elaboration, support or criticism of the arguments advanced. For instance in a discussion as to whether or not certain developments should be considered examples of progress or regress, a class might first discuss the meaning of 'progress' before moving on to apply the concept to history.

4: Pose problems and questions which genuinely reflect the difficulties encountered and the misconceptions held by the pupils themselves. Such problems may often seem unreal or contrived from the perspective of the professional historian. For instance 'Sources (32 page 25 and 168 page 93) both show horses being used to drive corn mills. Does this prove that the people in Source 168 must have learned about such mills from those in Source 32 (or does this prove that water-mills and windmills had not been invented at the time?).'

5: Try to reduce abstruse conceptual problems to simple questions. 'Core' questions capable of being posed over and over again with different material can be a very useful tool for the teacher. They need to be both accessible and sensible to the pupil.

Some examples of core questions
☆ Why are wrong ideas and useless developments sometimes important in history? How can they matter if they are wrong or useless?
☆ Why did some things have to be discovered more than once?
☆ Why do people persist with practices that are inefficient or that do more harm than good?
☆ Things often happen that nobody wanted, or things that many people want don't work out. Does this mean that people have no effect on history?
☆ If some bad effects for some people follow from every change, is there such a thing as 'progress'?
☆ If we say 'X was the cause of Y', does this mean that once X happened then Y was bound to happen?

D: Teachers should aim to develop pupils' thinking, not to produce 'good' written work.

There is agreement among educational researchers and HMIs that pupils of all abilities are often seriously underchallenged. This can be the result of teachers failing to pose questions to which clear-cut and complete answers are unlikely. Instead tasks are often restricted to those which elicit more-or-less competent and reasonable work. The appropriateness of the task is often judged by the quality of the end product, so that written work may rarely demand more than the exercise of skills which pupils are already known to possess. A better way to evaluate a task is to decide what pupils may learn from it. Some of the things they may learn are;
1: To apply past learning to new content
2: To identify exceptions to rules
3: To apply existing skills in new ways or to new material
4: To refine old skills or concepts or to develop new ones in the face of a new problem
5: That pupils' existing ideas don't work for all cases
6: That their existing ideas are internally inconsistent
7: That history is more difficult than they had thought

Only rarely will a pupil faced with a serious new challenge produce an adequate response on the first occasion. But from the weaknesses of this first response much can be learned. Indeed when a challenge produces an adequate response with no weaknesses it is time to raise the stakes with a more challenging task.

A task may be deemed inappropriate for five reasons;

1: It fails to challenge the pupils. Pupils have already demonstrated that tasks of this sort are well within their capacity, and they have nothing further to learn from them.
2: It tells the teacher nothing. A teacher needs to be able to tell what the pupils found difficult and what misconceptions they hold.
3: It leads nowhere. A task which has no intrinsic value may still be useful if it prepares the ground or acts as a stepping stone to a point of vantage from which some more productive exercise may be tackled.
4: Pupils learn nothing of value from it.
5: Pupils not properly equipped to tackle the task.

These five reasons could all be exemplified if, for instance a group of five pupils were set work on energy conservation with the following task.

'Make (Write, tape, or present orally to the class) an account of how methods of energy conservation have changed. You may not refer to more than ten main historical events or use more than six quotations from sources.' Pupils might by these restrictions be prevented from collecting together all they know. They will be forced to select facts which are significant within a line of development, and illustrations which are apposite. This is a demanding exercise and most pupils would probably make a mess of it. They might for instance select facts for ill-conceived reasons e.g. according to whether the conservation methods were similar to or different from those in use today. But this would be useful since it would give the teacher insight into their thinking and thus a point of reference for future teaching. The exercise would be inappropriate, however, if the pupils had already done an exactly similar exercise and merely replicated entirely satisfactory previous results. It would be equally unsatisfactory if pupils merely selected conservation methods at random, or failed to select at all, or were unable to understand the sources, to manage the tape-recorder, or to talk coherently to the class.

The book is designed round the strategy outlined in Scheme 1 on page 7 above. Teachers will wish to supplement it with other materials and activities—see lists of books, films, videos, slides, museums etc. on pages 52 to 57.

A: **The narrative** pages 7–88

The narrative section of the book serves five purposes;

1: To provide a first overview of events.
2: To arouse and maintain interest
3: To maintain the idea that history is an enquiry based on evidence.
4: To make enough sense of technical developments such as the steam engine, or economic changes such as the industrial revolution for pupils to see that these things are in principle explicable, and to be able to handle them as parts of the story.
5: To act as a reference when work is done on the later sections of the book. Items are included in the narrative as links to which later ideas or information may be attached. This guide lists these links in its treatment of each section of the narrative. A teacher may decide to use them to raise questions and to prepare links at an early stage, or alternatively may skip them completely in the first brief overview.

Selection by the teacher

Since the book is designed for pupils of a wide range of ability, teachers should be selective in its use.

In selecting material they should give first priority among the purposes listed above to overview and interest (a and b). The book is designed as far as possible in double page spreads, each concerned with one main idea that is indicated in the heading. It is suggested that even in a rapid overview pupils' attention should be directed to each double page, even if only to note the heading or refer to picture(s).

An outline of the 'story line' of the narrative will be found on page 8 above.

An outline of the 'story line' of each part of the narrative will be found under the heading 'Objectives' at the beginning of each narrative section of this 'Guide'. In this outline the absolute essentials have been underlined to help teachers with the problem of selection. It is suggested that these should be clearly recorded by the pupils as they use the narrative, so as to help them to distinguish between the durable and the disposable parts of the story.

At five points in the narrative, 3500 BC, AD 500, 1500, 1875 and the present, a short summary is given of the story so far. This is presented in visual as well as in written form, and is intended to help pupils to sift the durable from the disposable, as well as to help in building up overview.

The need for the teacher to select applies also to the sources.

It may be undesirable to interrupt the narrative flow by time-consuming source work. During the first overview a teacher may find sources useful mainly to illustrate or make clear by example the events of the narrative. The numbering of all sources should make it easy to come back to them for particular evaluation or synthesis exercises when the teacher sees that these are needed. All sources, visual or written have been given a number for ease of reference in exercises. Some pictures which are simply illustrations have not been given a source number, but since virtually anything could be seen as a historical source for some purpose, this decision is inevitably arbitrary.

A note on sources

Wherever necessary sources have been adapted to make them as accessible as possible to pupils of 14–16. Sentences have been shortened, spellings modernised or modern words substituted, and no attempt has been made to indicate omissions. Many sources are in any case translations from a foreign language, and all are tiny selections made with a specific purpose from much larger materials. At an appropriate point in their work in evaluating sources teachers might encourage pupils to discuss the problems of authenticity and reliability raised by this adaptation.

Use of questions

The questions printed in the pupils' book are intended to indicate possible lines of thought while leaving readers to solve problems for themselves. They are not intended as exercises or as invitations to class discussion. Teachers may wish to use them where they fit into the purpose in hand, but should not allow them to interrupt the narrative in stage 1.

B: Factors pages 89–140

The material in this section is not put forward as a set of 'correct' factors, which when multiplied together in some way produced the historical events. It is intended to provide a series of reasonably sized topics from which a teacher may select one or two, or more for more able pupils, to be used after the narrative with the aim of consolidating overview and starting pupils thinking in causal terms.

When events which might form part of a factor have been dealt with by more than passing reference in the narrative, material is not repeated in the factor section. It is assumed that teachers will begin a factor by picking up threads from the narrative and that pupils will frequently refer back to the narrative pages.

The material in the factors section varies in difficulty, and teachers will wish to use them selectively. 'War' and 'Transport' have been placed first, since they are the most concrete and require pupils to grasp few complex ideas. 'Conservation' 'Government' and 'Ideas' will be found more challenging.

Teachers may wish to use sources or other material from one of the 'factors' independently to strengthen part of the narrative or to exemplify one of the problems.

Teacher may wish to use other factors than those chosen by the author. See suggestions on page 29.

C: Problems pages 141–170

The problems, like the factors, are designed to lead back into the earlier sections at many points. Apart from 'People' and 'Why Did it Happen Then?' the problem chapters have very little independent substance. They are essentially maps to help pupils to think about the material in the narrative and factors sections.

This last section of the book is, however of great importance, since the main aim of the course is to encourage pupils to develop their thinking about problems of this type. Some items within it are disposable, and teachers might find other material elsewhere to exemplify the same points. But some work should be done on each of the main chapters. Although difficult issues are raised most of the questions are accessible at a relatively simple level. Work on problems of this type is likely to be a useful part of examination revision in year 5, since these are essentially the same problems round which the new SHP 'Energy through Time' syllabuses of the Examinations Boards are centred.

4: Teaching the narrative

1: The introduction
pages 7–8

A: Objectives

After having used this section pupils should:

1: Be able to explain how energy use is important to them personally.
2: Be able to draw the contrast between our present energy-rich society and those of earlier societies and of 'low energy' societies today.
3: Have some idea that energy takes various forms–fuel, electricity, animal power.
4: Have some idea that consumer goods have an 'energy cost'–that is that energy is needed to make them.

B: Discussion points

Material included under this heading is intended to suggest a range of ideas to teachers or to arm them against problems that may arise in class discussion. Some of the points might be made the basis of exercises or of a formally organised discussion. Many of the points will not be appropriate for some groups.

1: Discussion of the modern high energy world.
a) What methods of energy use are shown in the picture on page seven.
Guesses based on costs are likely to be the

only response. Averages from 'Which?'
September 1982:

Domestic space heating   Used 63.3% of fuel
Domestic hot water   Used 22%
Cooking   Used 10%
Appliances   Used 4.7%

In Britain in 1979 we used 27% of our energy in the home, 37% in industry and 23% in transport.

b) What other methods common today are not shown in the picture?
c) Which uses most?
d) What fuels are used to produce the energy uses shown?
e) Which (which 3?) items shown in the picture needed most energy to produce them?

Again guesses based on cost are likely to be the only starting point. Energy is used at every stage of the production of almost everything. See Figure A.

Figure A

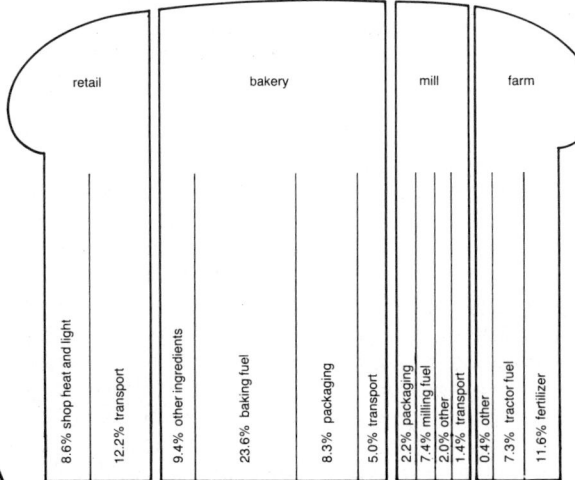

The detailed breakdown of the fuel cost of a standard white loaf. The total fuel cost is 5.6 kWht/loaf.

The following table, based on Chapman 'Fuel's Paradise' page 56–7, takes the amount of energy needed to make one loaf as a unit. This amount is 4kwh (including, of course, a large percentage of energy that is wasted).

Item	Energy cost
Loaf	1
House	17900
Car	4000
Washing machine	375
Colour TV	1232
Transistor radio	77
Jumbo jet	3571000
Plastic per kilo	8
Steel per kilo	2.3
Aluminum per kilo	4.7

2: Discussion of the low energy worlds of the past, or of other regions today.

Same questions as in 1 above.

In both sources 1 and 2 the ploughshare would certainly be of iron, though this is not very clearly shown. Domestic interiors of both these times and places would certainly include pots, some metal objects and wood fuel.

3: Discussion of the contrast between the different societies.

a) When and why has it come about?

This is the $64000 question of energy history, and worth at any rate opening up at this stage.

b) Is today's uneven distribution of energy 'fair'?

Another large and very woolly question, but a fairly accessible one which opens interesting ideas.

C: **Difficulties and further information**

Material included under this heading throughout this Guide is intended to forewarn teachers of possible conceptual confusions, or to provide them with further background information.

1: The fact that electricity is not a fuel, but a way of transmitting energy produced at the power station, may cause some confusion, but this should lead to a useful distinction. Some pupils will not know that power stations can be driven by coal, oil or nuclear energy or by water-power. N.B. Hydro-electric power is not a use of fuel, but a conversion of energy from one form to another like the solar panel on the house across the road in the picture.

2: 'Energy Slaves'. The cartoon is merely a graphic metaphor, and has no scientific precision. The number 85 was calculated by taking the amount of energy produced in UK per person per day in 1981 (113 kwh), assuming that 50% of it was wasted, and dividing the result by the amount of energy which an imaginary slave would produce in an eight-hour day (.6kwh).

2: Fire and the hunter
pages 10–11

A: **Objectives**

After using this section pupils should:

1: Know that

a) Man discovered (rather than invented) fire about 500,000 years ago. This was his first artificial source of energy.

b) Fire made life safer by enabling people to:

i) survive in cold areas
ii) cook
iii) make better tools and weapons.
iv) gain some safety from predators
c) Socially fire enhanced the unity of human groups.

d) In order to master fire people had to:
i) learn how to keep it alive.
ii) learn how to light it.
2: Be aware that we share some attitudes with these early ancestors. Fire is still a potent symbol of 'hearth and home'.

B: Discussion points:

1: The discovery of fire.
Which was the most significant discovery:
a) the existence of fire.
b) method of using fire
c) methods of control of fire?
(See also Exercise 3 below)

2: What difference did fire make to the lives of the hunter/gatherers?
a) What old problems did it solve?
b) What new problems did it create?
3: What would be the feelings, fears, etc of the human group if and when their fire 'died'? (note the word. What does it imply?)
4: What, if anything, would seem as wonderful to us as fire to early man? (The arrival of Martians? Winning the Pools?)
5: What sort of evidence do we have on these matters and how reliable are our conclusions? (see also Exercise 4 below on this question)

Figure B

Time scales:
Peking Man lived about half a million years ago. If the time since then was squashed into one day of 24 hours. . . .

`00·01·00`

. . . Iron was first made about 10 minutes (3500 years) ago.

`23·50·00`

`12·00·00`

. . . The first successful steam engine was made 47 seconds ago (in the year 1711).

`23·59·13`

. . . People like us (homo sapiens) first appeared about 3 hours (60,000 years) ago.

`21·00·00`

. . . An old person aged 70 was born 12 seconds ago.

`23·59·48`

. . . The first farmers began to grow crops only half an hour (10,000 years) ago.

`23·30·00`

. . . A fifteen year-old was born 2.6 seconds ago.

`23·59·57`

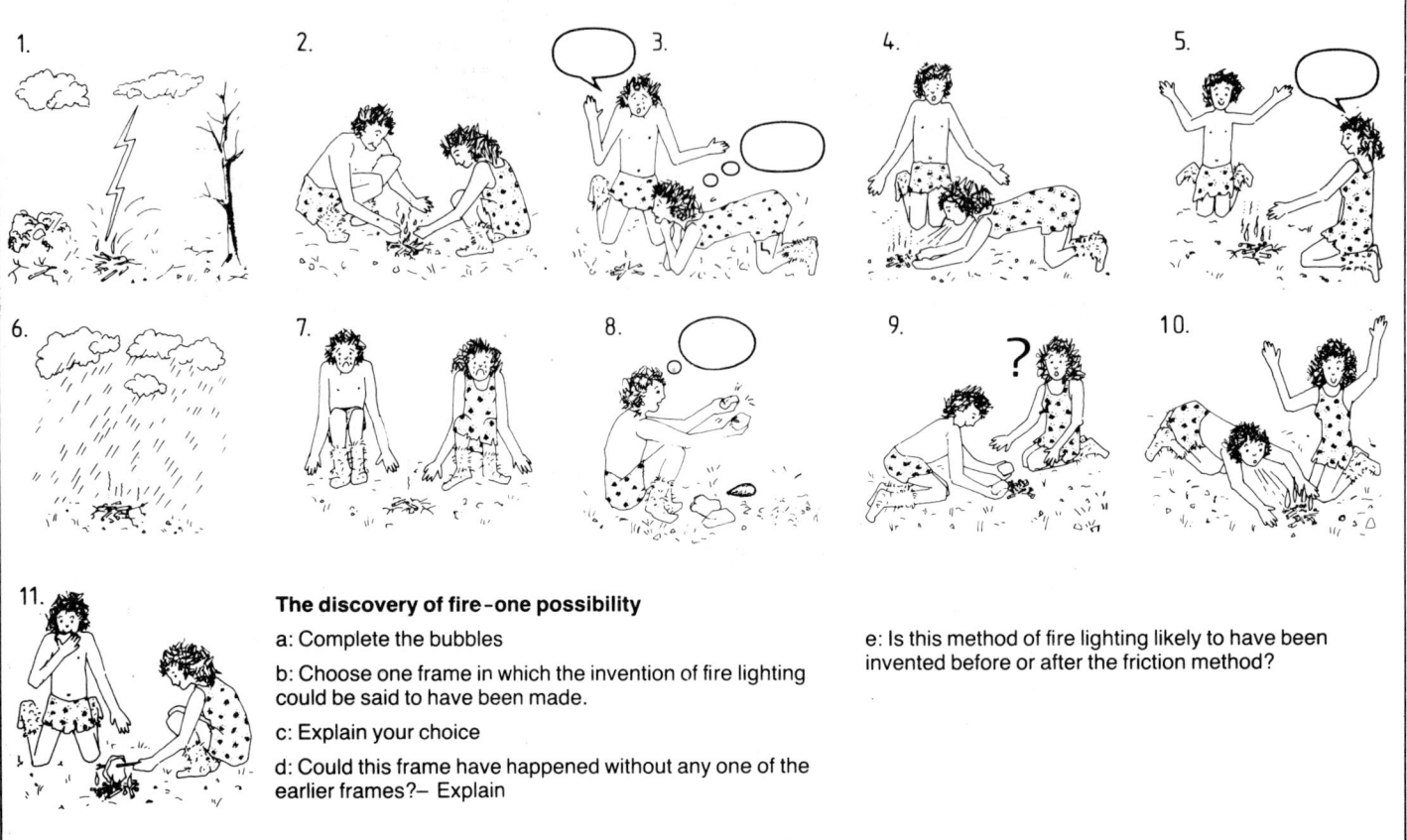

The discovery of fire – one possibility

a: Complete the bubbles

b: Choose one frame in which the invention of fire lighting could be said to have been made.

c: Explain your choice

d: Could this frame have happened without any one of the earlier frames? – Explain

e: Is this method of fire lighting likely to have been invented before or after the friction method?

Figure C

C: **Difficulties and further information**

Chronology

500 000 is much too large a number to make much sense to most pupils. Some sort of clock face or time-line device is needed. The idea that for most of the Old Stone Age change happened with imperceptible slowness is one of importance, and an awareness of the enormous amounts of time involved helps to establish this. The relationship of the speed of change to the length of human life and memory is of obvious importance. At 25 years to a generation, Peking Man is our great, great. . . 12 500 times great. . . grandfather. (see Figure B).

The point might also be made by getting the class to sit silently for first one second, to represent the time since the end of the palaeolithic, and then for 50 seconds, to represent the time since Peking Man. Another method is to take the class outside, and space markers out at one pace for 500 years. The Norman Conquest is 2 paces from the present and Peking man 1000.

D: **Activities**

A: Make a fire drill and try to light a fire with it. It is easy enough to produce a good deal of heat, but the attempt to produce fire is likely to fail. This is worthwhile if only to enhance respect for the skill of early man, and for hard work. (See exercise 4 below) Using an electric drill enough friction can be generated fairly easily to show that it works.

B: Sharpen and harden a stick by burning the end. Scrape off the loose carbon. Try to sharpen a similar stick without burning – using a flint? Compare.

E: **Exercises**

The 'Exercise' sections throughout this guide are intended to suggest ideas to teachers rather than to prescribe what they should do or in any way to put forward a balanced programme for pupils. Many more exercises are included in the early parts of the Guide than in later parts because of the need to establish exemplars of exercise types, which the teacher may then transfer to other contexts. Many ideas from the exercises could easily be adapted to form the basis of discussion or of group or individual work.

1: *(See Figure C)*

(The purpose of this exercise is to encourage empathetic thinking in a carefully controlled context, and to help pupils to see that changes arise not out of the blue, but out of a set of pre-conditions. This logical idea can perhaps be seen most easily in a context where there is very little actual evidence to confuse us. At the same time we should be clear that though speculations such as those based on he cartoon may be historical thinking, they cannot, without solid evidence, become history.)

2: Fire was used in the Old Stone Age for
i) warmth

ii) cooking
iii) to make tools
iv) to keep off wild beasts.
Place these uses in the order in which you think they were discovered. Explain your reasons. (All these uses are shown in the picture on page 7, which could be used as the basis for the exercise. If pupils individually or in small groups choose an order, then whole class discussion to arbitrate between the various possibilities must necessarily involve empathetic reconstruction of the problems and perspectives of stone age people.)

3: From the evidence used in this section choose the piece which you consider to be the *most reliable* and the piece you consider to be the *least* reliable. Explain the reasons for your choice.

4: ***Attempt to light a fire using Iron Age techniques.***

'How were they to light the new fire? They had practiced vigorously with the fire drill. . . one person presses down while the other saws away vigorously with the bow. Within a few seconds the bow wears away a little depression. . . within a minute or two there (should be) a strong smell of scorching and with luck a thin plume of woodsmoke. Theoretically, or so the books maintain, the sawdust in the hole then ignites and can be transferred to a tinder of dry hay or wood shavings. Armed with all this information Peter Little sawed away at the fire drill. And sawed. And sawed. After half an hour he was ready to give up. 'I think there's more smoke under my armpits than in that fire drill,' he observed.

'I've seen Australian aborigines do it in 30 seconds, 'said Sarah unhelpfully. Fortunately there was a friendly tribe of field cameramen with a cigarette lighter on hand to kindle the fire.'

(From J. Percival *'Living in the Past'* BBC 1980 p. 47)
a) This source describes events in the 1970s, when BBC TV arranged for a group of people to live for a year in Iron Age conditions. Can we draw from it any reliable conclusions about the fire technology used by people in the Iron Age, 2000 years ago?
b) Can we draw conclusion about people in the Stone Age?

(Further questioning about *how* such conclusions may be possible should lead to the idea of continuity–some things, like physical conditions, stay the same.)

F: **Links with factors and problems**

Material included under this heading in the Guide is intended to help teachers to build connections during the later stages of the course. But they may find it useful to erect signposts at an early stage, or to begin then to build up an idea that is to be reinforced later.

1: The idea of invention is one that will recur time and again throughout this study. The question 'Who invented x?', though interesting, is not a very fruitful one historically. The first appearance of an idea is likely to be far less important than its first application at a time when it fits into a social and economic context–when 'the time is ripe' for it. Thus fire is likely to have been discovered independently in many places and at many times before people with the necessary intelligence and social organisation used it to change their 'way of life'.

2: Craftsmanship and technical skill. To make a fire drill which worked was a great feat of skill and insight. Even in a simple society with little or no specialisation, the special skills of some individuals must have marked them out. Later the skilled craftsmanship of metal worker, millwright, engine-minder, were to be merged in the engineer. In a world which had no 'scientific' explanation for anything, the skill and success of the craftsman was to be explained in terms of magic and mystery. See 'Ideas' page 131 for Prometheus and other fire myths.

3: Eternal fire. See 'Ideas' pages 131, 132, 140 for altar fires, vestal virgins, and Olympic flames which perhaps represent in later periods the vital importance of keeping fire alive.

4: Fuel problem – important in most other periods of history, but notable here by its absence. In treeless regions, like Siberia there was in fact a fuel problem, solved by palaeolithic hunters burning bones. But in general, nomadic hunters, unlike all settled populations, can have had little need to bring fuel from a distance and so no real fuel problem.

5: Use of fire to make something. The fire-hardened sticks and antlers of the palaeolithic are not quite an industrial use in the everyday usage of the word, but they are the first item in a series of uses of fire that includes industrial uses such as pottery, metals and much of the modern chemical and plastics industry.

6: A technical advance usually sets new problems. Once man became dependent on fire it was urgently important to learn how to light it. Similarly dependence on coal made it urgently important to improve pumps, hence steam engines. This has obvious relevance to the idea of progress.

7: The option of abandoning a technical advance is not normally available. (again relevant to progress) Once man became used to fire he could hardly do without, especially those people who had used fire to enable them to live in cold climates, such as that of Britain–or Peking.

3: The first energy revolution

A: Objectives

After having used this section pupils should know that;

1: Agriculture began about 10,000 years ago. This led to the first large increase in needs for and supply of energy–the first 'Energy Revolution'

2: It led to needs for energy:
a) to till, reap etc. in fields.
b) to grind corn.
c) to bake brew etc.
d) to make pots.

3: Fuel supply became a problem for static villages because of these extra needs, though usually an easily soluble one.
4: Energy was now needed to transport fuel and agricultural produce.
5: Animals became available as a source of energy.

They should also begin to be aware that the fuel 'problem' is closely connected with transport and its 'costs'.

B: Discussion points

1: How far is it worth going to fetch fire-wood on foot?
(Experience with bonfires may be relevant)
(Source 152 page 86 might be used)
a) How much can one person carry?
b) What factors would neolithic people have to consider? (Time that could be spared, urgency of fuel need)

2: What is it like to have to work steadily at a physical task for hours on end? Has anybody in the class done it?
3: How might animals have first been trained to work?
4: In what ways were the changes described in this chapter important? (See below 'difficulties'. See also Exercise 1 below)
5: What explanation might be offered for the fact that these changes happen first where they did?

C: Difficulties and further information

1: Urban children may find it difficult to see how much of our familiar world goes back to the 'neolithic revolution'. The differences between our world and that of the early farmers are much more obvious than the similarities. But agriculture is still our basic food source, the plough is still a 'master tool', pottery is still an essential craft, transport of fuel is still vital. In a way only the details have changed.

2: The term 'Energy Revolution'. The term 'Revolution' will cause some difficulty. The fact the labels like 'Revolution' are stickers attached by historians rather than things which objectively existed, might usefully emerge from discussion. Teachers might point out when dealing with the next chapter (on the coming of urban societies) that the changes dealt with there followed on continuously from those of the neolithic, and that the first energy revolution can be said to stretch over several thousand years. Since the context out of which it emerged is the half million years since Peking Man, it was can still be said to have happened at revlutionary speed.
(See also F6 below)

D: Activities

An 'Energy slaves' calculation might be attempted (with due emphasis on the vagueness of any figures.) Draught animals are reasonably easy. An ox can do about seven times as much work as a man, and a donkey about twice as much, (see table page 149). However animals do only certain types of work, and probably a good deal of their time just eating and chewing the cud. Also the animals had to be looked after and fed.

An imaginary village might have 50 families, 200 people, 10 working oxen and 10 donkeys. If each animal worked a fifth of the total time the equivalent would be 20 'men'. Even making no allowance for man-power used up in tending the work-beasts, this would only be one tenth of an 'Energy slave' for each person.

Firewood is much more difficult and best left out of account, since most of the energy in it was wasted, and a good deal was spent in fetching it. A modern peasant family of six using wood fuel may use about 10kg a day. (G Foley 'Energy in the transition from Rural Subsistence' 1982) The energy in this is equivalent to 38.3 kwh, but probably 99% of this is wasted. A man can produce .6 kwh in 8 hours of steady work. If a neolithic family of four used and wasted about the same amount as Foley's modern peasants they would each have another one tenth of an 'Energy slave' at their disposal. (1% of 38.3 divided by 4=.095) Most pupils will only be confused by an attempt at this stage to equate the energy in fuel with that used in doing work, but bright ones might learn from trying to think numerically about the neolithic village. The exercise would only be really useful as part of a general plan to produce a graph of 'energy slaves' after having completed the narrative. A teacher might decide to return to this after the development of the steam engine had been used to convince pupils that the heat energy of fuel could be turned into mechanical power.

E: Exercises

1: a) Make two lists:
i) A list of the energy needs of neolithic people.
ii) A list of the sources of energy available to neolithic people.
b) Place a tick beside each item on either list which also applied in the Old Stone Age. (For a very weak group lists could be provided with two columns for ticks.)
c) Place another tick beside each item that still applies in Britain today.

d) How important was the coming of farming for the history of energy through time?
(Able pupils might tackle part d) without the guidance.)

2: Animals were used by the early farmers for various tasks. Look at the following list:
a) Ploughing (source 12)
b) Treading in seed (source 11a)
c) Carrying loads on their backs (source 11b)
d) Dragging loads behind them
e) Threshing grain (source 11c)
f) Giving milk or wool
g) Giving meat or leather
i) Put this list in the order in which these things may have been invented or discovered.
ii) Give reasons for your choice.
iii) Could the order have been different?

3: If you were an archaeologist how might the following evidence help you to decide whether a site you were investigating had been inhabited by farmers?

Animal bones
Remains of tools
Remains of pots
Remains of buildings. (Buildings or pits used for grain storage?)

(A more difficult version – with no guidance list – 'How could you tell whether the site was an agricultural one?')

4: Divide the sources used in this chapter into two groups:
a) Those which actually come from the time of the earliest farmers.
b) Those which come from later periods.
How certain can we be of conclusions about the earlier period drawn from group b)?

F: **Links with factors and problems**

1: The idea of hard, laborious physical work. This has been the lot of most farming people (i.e. most people) since neolithic times, and is a necessary background against which to view the introduction of labour and energy saving techniques in later parts of the narrative.

2: The relationship of transport to fuel availability is to be a constant factor. The circle from which the neolithic farmer could bring fire-wood is the first of a series of widening circles, ending with the world fuel market of the 20th century (see *Transport* pages 97–108).

3: The pottery kiln is one of a long series of industrial uses of energy. It could reach high temperatures and is therefore very likely to be the ancestor of the metal-worker's furnace, and of all other industrial furnaces.

4: Animal energy, which begins to be harnessed in this period, is to be the only motive power available until the invention of the water-mill, and the main one in agriculture until the 20th century.

5: Progress. Do things get better? Farming is heavier and more boring work than hunting. (Ask a 19th century Plains Indian or a Lincolnshire poacher). The solution of the problem of food production led to a host of new problems e.g. storage and cooking, hence pottery. There are many other examples of the fact that the solution of a technical problem, instead of leading to the dawning of the millennium simply poses another series of problems.

6: Energy revolutions. This idea is taken up in the use of the term 'Second Energy Revolution' for the transition that began with the Industrial Revolution, and further material is to be found in 'Trends and Turning Points' pages 146–152.

3: The low energy civilisations 3500 BC–AD 500
pages 17–28

A: **Objectives**

After using this section pupils should:
1: Know that during these four milleniums a series of regional civilisations arose in different parts of the world. With their relatively heavily populated areas and complex social and economic organisations they faced a series of energy problems:
i) Fuel supply
ii) Energy was needed for the production of metals.
iii) Transport (partly of fuel) needed energy. New techniques were developed to harness animals, wind and water for transport.
iv) Organised war led to the development of ways of using the horse.
v) Energy was needed to operate some machines, in particular corn mills and irrigation devices.

This need was at first met by slavery and animal power, but later led to the first artificial 'Prime mover' or source of mechanical power, the water mill.

2: Grasp the continuity between these changes and those discussed in the previous chapter 'The first Energy Revolution'. The city meant a continuation of the rapid expansion of needs for and sources of energy begun with the cooking of agriculture.

3: Be aware that the whole world is the area of the 'Study in Development'. The map showing regional areas of civilisation is designed to do this, and to raise questions about the spread of ideas. It can be linked with later world maps showing the world energy market etc.

4: Understand the concept of a 'Prime Mover'. The history of energy is given one of its shapes by the development in turn of a series of prime movers. Pupils will at this stage be able to suggest the later members of this series (Wind mill, steam engine, internal combustion engine). It is useful to establish the general concept when the first of the series appear (Animal powered mills and water mills).

B: **Discussion points**

1: Did techniques spread from one place of origin or were they independently invented in various places? This question might help to establish the 'world area', and to give a shape to this long and rather artificial period.

Some relevant evidence is to be found on the Time chart and the map, in the dates given for various developments, such as chariots and water mills. (See below C2 for discussion of this and exercise 1 below).

2: What was the importance of transport (or war, or government action) in the history of energy in this period?

3: Why were there no water mills till about 100 BC?

Grinding corn had been a steady chore for nearly 9000 years. The potter's wheel and the wheeled vehicle had been known for nearly 4000 years. There had been plenty of skilled craftsmen in stone, metal and wood for about the same length of time. So why were there no water mills till c. 100 BC? (See below C3 for discussion)

4: Why did the Romans make so little use of water mills? (raises some of the same issues as 3 above, but also questions of rainfall (see source 20 page 112)

C: **Difficulties and further information**

1: The mechanical working of water mills may cause problems for some. See suggestions about models in D below. The completely unmechanical could be assured that it is only necessary to know that water running downhill did the work.

2: Diffusion or separate development of inventions. The radically different design of Chinese from western water lifting machines, may indicate a different origin.

The transmission of techniques between western Asia and the Mediterranean civilisations is very obvious. The only clear conclusion possible from the evidence given is the priority of Mesopotamia. The isolation of the American civilisations is clear from the map. The fact that there were no draught animals, wheeled vehicles, or bronze or iron working in America until Europeans brought them there is not mentioned at this point in the text, but would be useful in any discussion of the transmission of techniques.

The most interesting problems arise in connection with the links between western Asia

and China. The sudden and complete appearance in China, about 2000 BC, of a civilisation with advanced metallurgy, chariots etc may indicate contacts either overland or by sea. Links between the Roman World and China were well established. The best Roman steel was imported from China, as well as silk. Useful map in Times Atlas of World History page 71. Han China (roughly Roman period) was technologically in advance of the West.

3: Why no water mills till c. 100BC? To a 'mechanically minded' age like ours, it seems strange that this useful invention was so long delayed. (See Exercise 2 below for the hard grind of the hand mill).

An answer quite likely to occur to children who have just read the Homer passage (Source 19 page 20) is that the work was done by women or slaves and men and rich people didn't worry too much about how hard they had to work. This is clearly part of the answer. But another problem for the teacher is to get modern children, to whom the idea of mechanical power is utterly familiar, to enter into a world where it was quite unknown, where work was done, either by people or animals, or else by gods or devils. (See Source 36 page 26, where Antipater of Thessalonica makes just this assumption.) The idea is difficult, but some of our pupils are certainly capable of grasping it. If the idea that the mental furniture of people of a different time and place was very different from ours is established with a clear example like this, it can be reinforced as other examples recur.

D: **Activities**

1: Models. One working model of a machine such as a mill is worth hours of talk and diagrams. Pupils with construction kits or practical skills or colleagues teaching Design and Technology might be able to help. 'Lego-Technic' materials may be available in the Technology Department. The main conceptual problem is probably with the gearing as in the Saqiya (page 25) and the Vitruvian mill (page 26)

2: An energy slave's calculation might be based on the following source:

What is needed to equip a vineyard

The slave overseer with his wife, 10 workmen, one ox driver, one ass driver, one to provide the willows, one swineherd, 16 in all. Also two oxen, two asses to pull carts and one ass for the mill. Also three presses and jars enough for the wine. Also two wagons, two ploughs, harness and other things.

(Cato 'On Agriculture' Rome c. 175 BC)

If Cato had lived on the vineyard, he would have had domestic slaves as well. Cato was in no sense typical, but it is of some interest to see what energy resources a rich Roman might command.

See above (page 16) for discussion of such calculations, or table (page 149) for figures.

3: Make and/or use a model hand mill? Two flattish pieces of hard stone and a few handfuls of rice or barley might give some idea of the amount of labour involved in producing enough flour to sustain life. (see also Exercise 2 below)

E: **Exercises**

1: a) Construct a Time Chart showing the development and spread of new ways of using energy 3500 BC–AD 500.
b) What ideas about how inventions spread from one region to another might be based on this evidence?
c) How can you decide which of these ideas is likely to be correct?

2: Read the following passage. It comes from the account of an experiment in which modern people as part of a BBC TV programme lived an Iron Age way of life for a year, using hand mills to grind their corn.

'The flour mills spun intermittently all day long. It was one of the most characteristic sounds in the village, a rather soothing, scraping, sawing sound as the stones turned. A hand-mill is basically nothing more than one stone sitting on top of another. The grain is trickled down through a hole in the top, so that it is trapped between the underside of the upper stone and the top of the one beneath. As the upper stone turns the trapped grain is crushed into flour. It is slow heavy work. Early in the year the couple responsible for baking the bread on a particular day also had to grind a day's supply of grain, but this placed an unduly heavy burden on the bakers. So a new procedure was worked out whereby everyone in the village had to grind two bowls full of wheat every day.'
(J Percival. *'Living in the Past.'* BBC 1980)

These hand mills were of the rotary type used in Iron Age Britain. The upper stone was turned round and round instead of being moved backwards and forwards like the Greek one shown on page 21.)
a) Were things the same or different for the people in this experiment compared with people using similar hand-mills in ancient times:
i) In the actual work?
ii) In their attitude to it?
iii) In the arrangements made for getting it done? (What other arrangements – women? slaves? – might have been used in ancient times?)
b) What historical value has evidence of this sort?
   (The main reason for including this source is to emphasise the hard and continual labour needed in early agricultural societies.
   See Activities D3 above.)

3: Source 25 page 22 (Hammurabi letter)
a) How many freighters were in use? (124)
b) What can we tell from this source about iron working in Babylon?
c) How reliable is this source?

4: Source 18 page 20 (Herodotus)

a) What can we tell from this passage about the strength of the Egyptian government?
b) How much reliance can be placed on Herodotus's evidence?
   Read also sources 19 and 20 pages 20 and 21 (Homer, Diodorus)
c) What conclusions can be drawn from these three pieces of evidence about the importance of slavery in the ancient world?
d) Does this show that people living in ancient times were more brutal and unfeeling than we are today?

5: Look at Source 29 (Ramses II picture page 24)
a) Why should a painting like this be made in the King's tomb?
b) Is this painting likely to be an accurate record of actual events?
c) What parts of the picture are likely to be i) most accurate ii) least accurate? Give reasons for your choice.

6: You are a Roman starting a new bakery about 100 AD. You need freshly ground flour every day. You have to decide how to grind it. The choices are:
a) build a water mill,
b) build a donkey mill,
c) employ slaves to work hand mills.
i) What will you need to know before you can choose? (Cost of buying and feeding slaves or donkeys, cost of building or repairing mills, regular availability of water supply, donkey food, slave food.)
ii) Which is the safest choice?
iii) Why?

F: **Links with factors and problems**

1: Water mill as the first inanimate prime mover

2: Horse harness. The horse was not used for any serious traction in any of the ancient civilisations, but for light work and above all for speed. The harness, copied from that of the real beast of burden, the ox, was so designed that heavy traction tended to throttle the horse. This throat harness is seen in the chariot picture page 24. The next section takes up this idea, and there are some relevant sources and pictures under 'Transport'. (especially page 99)

3: Problem of lifting water in the mines – see source from Diodorus page 21. This was to recur in pressing form in 16th/17th. century Europe when it lead directly to the steam engine.

4: Government control of limited energy source – see Hammurabi Source 25 page 22. Lord of Manor and water power or State energy controls today, as developed in the 'Government' factor.

5: War. If an energy source has a military value its development takes a high priority. Chariots, metals, c.f. H bombs.

6: Conservation and energy shortages. No real evidence supplied in the narrative, but see 'Shortage and Conservation' pages 111–12.

Transport development usually enabled the early cities to solve their problems without too much trauma. The fact that the city solved its energy problem by bringing in supplies of fuel (and energy-rich goods like iron) from a much wider circle than did the village, anticipates the parallel fact that the industrial state solves its similar problems by bringing fuel etc from a world energy market. This pattern of widening circles raises the world fuel problem, since the world is of finite size. More on this in 'Transport' pages 97–107 and 'Conservation' pages 108–21. Although the evidence is not very precise it is suggested (M Wheeler–'The Civilisations of the Indus Valley and Beyond') that the Indus Civilisation, which disappeared rather abruptly about 1250 BC may have done so partly becaus it outran its fuel supply. There is a good deal of anecdotal evidence of the destruction of forest around the Mediterranean in ancient times, probably as much by goats and for agriculture as for fuel. Attempts, not very conclusive, have been made to link this with climatic change and with the economic decline of the Mediterranean world after AD200. The fact that the Mediterranean world was short of energy in the two most easily available forms of wood and water power is certainly a point of interest. The contrast with Europe in the Middle Ages (next section) is sharp.

7: Hard work. The Odyssey source page 20 is used to emphasise the grinding (note the word) chore of hard physical work. The point has already been raised in connection with early farm work, and will recur often e.g. Source 143 page 78.

4: Low energy civilisations AD 500–1500
pages 29–35

A: **Objectives**

After having used this section pupils should:

1: Know that:
During the first half of this period Asian, mainly Chinese, technology was in the lead, as shown by
a) use of water power
b) improvement in ships
c) improvements in horse harness and stirrups
d) gunpowder
e) the new prime mover, the wind mill

2: Be able to identify factors which assist and inhibit the spread of technology. (e.g. transport links, warlike contact, geographical barriers, lack of socio-economic infrastructure)

B: **Discussion points**
1: Why do some ideas spread more rapidly than others? (e.g. stirrups rapidly, improved ships slowly)

2: Why do ideas spread rapidly at some times compared with others (e.g. Europe before and after c. 1100)?

3: How does the speed of the spread of ideas in the Middle Ages compare with a) prehistoric times b) the twentieth century? Why was it in comparison so slow or rapid?

4: What energy resources made Europe so rich and powerful at the end of the Middle Ages?

C: **Difficulties and further information**

1: Pupils may find it hard to see that ideas which are perfectly obvious to those who are familiar with them are nevertheless difficult when they are unfamiliar. Both the stirrups and the horse collar are examples of this. There is some danger that pupils might conclude that people in those days were just stupid. The fact that we advance into the future like sleep-walkers groping our way, is one that pupils will need help with, obvious though it is when pointed out.

2: One rather awkward question which thoughful pupils might raise is 'What happened to the Chinese technology towards the end of this period?' This question is perhaps more likely when they have completed the narrative with its account of the enormous developments of European technology since the Middle Ages. Whatever happened to China's technological lead? The likely answers seem to lie in the nature of Chinese government and society, the determination of the administrators of a highly centralised carefully balanced and largely self-contained civilisation to withstand disruptive change. Since pupils are likely to know very little about Chinese history little worthwhile discussion is possible. Teachers will find an interesting discussion of some of these issues in J Needham 'The Legacy of China' (OUP 1964).

D: **Activities**

1: Models. As with the water mill, the windmill could be made comprehensible much more easily by the use of models than by diagrams and talk.

2: An energy slaves calculation might be attempted for Salwarpe (Source 51 page 32). The salt-pans would have used a great deal of wood, as would domestic needs and the village blacksmith, and it would be very difficult to quantify these. So, though wood fuel might be discussed, it would have to be excluded from calculations. (See discussion above, page 16) Ideas about the number of plough beasts might be based on source 39 page 29, though probably many of these were only put to work at certain times of the year. See page 149 for table with useful figures for amounts of work. The population of Salwarpe might be arrived at by using a multiplier (4?) based on probable family size.

3: Dramatised simulation of argument for and against introducing horses instead of oxen in a medieval village. Class or group discussion might prepare arguments based on the likely interests of the following people:

a) Rich peasants (Have enough land to grow the necessary oats. Have corn to take to mill and hay etc. to carry home. Make regular trips to market.)

b) Poor peasants (can only grow enough grain for themselves. Need cattle for milk and meat. Share with each other in plough teams of four beasts at ploughing time.)

c) Miller (Mill depends on transport of corn in and flour out. Miller has rent of £3 a year to pay)

d) Lord of Manor's Reeve (has to provide horses for the Lord's use. Has to see that farming work on Lord's land is done efficiently)

e) Carter, blacksmith, harness-maker etc.

f) Landlord of village ale-house (Teacher's role? – Chairs discussion)

E: **Exercises**

1: Look at the map on pages 30 and 31, and at the table 'Energy inventions in the Middle Ages.' The dates are those of the earliest evidence, usually from China.

a) Does this mean that those inventions must have first been made in China and then spread from there?

b) Where else might stirrups have been invented? Explain your reasons.

c) Which inventions may well have been made independently in Europe? Explain your reasons.

d) Why should some inventions spread more quickly than others?

2: Draw a time chart of the energy changes 500–1500 AD.

3: (See Figure D) The diagram shows how some developments of Europe in the later Middle Ages helped to cause others. For instance a line joins 'Improved metal working' to 'Improved use of horses' because the extra metal meant that horse-shoes were easily available.

a) Choose another of the connections shown in the diagram and explain it.

b) One connecting line has been left out on purpose. Draw it in, and explain what the connection was. (Mills-metal link omitted)

4: Read Source 54 page 33. Use the information about the Abbot of Glastonbury (also page 33) to explain Abbot Samson's attitude to the new mill.

F: **Links with factors and problems**

1: The material about horses and about gunpowder and guns is more fully developed in the 'War' factor pages 90–96.

2: The importance of the move from oxen to horses is brought out more fully in 'Transport' pages 97–107. The horse was to be essential as the only readily available source of portable energy until the coming of the internal combustion engine.

3. The Abbot of Glastonbury's mill (page 33) is the first precise example in the book of the investment of capital. This idea is to become important in the 18th century and later, and the opportunity might be taken here to note what the abbot was doing, and to consider what sort of return he was getting. When, later in the narrative, Roebuck and Boulton invest in the steam engine, and it becomes more useful to talk of 'capital', the general idea will already be a little familiar.

Figure D

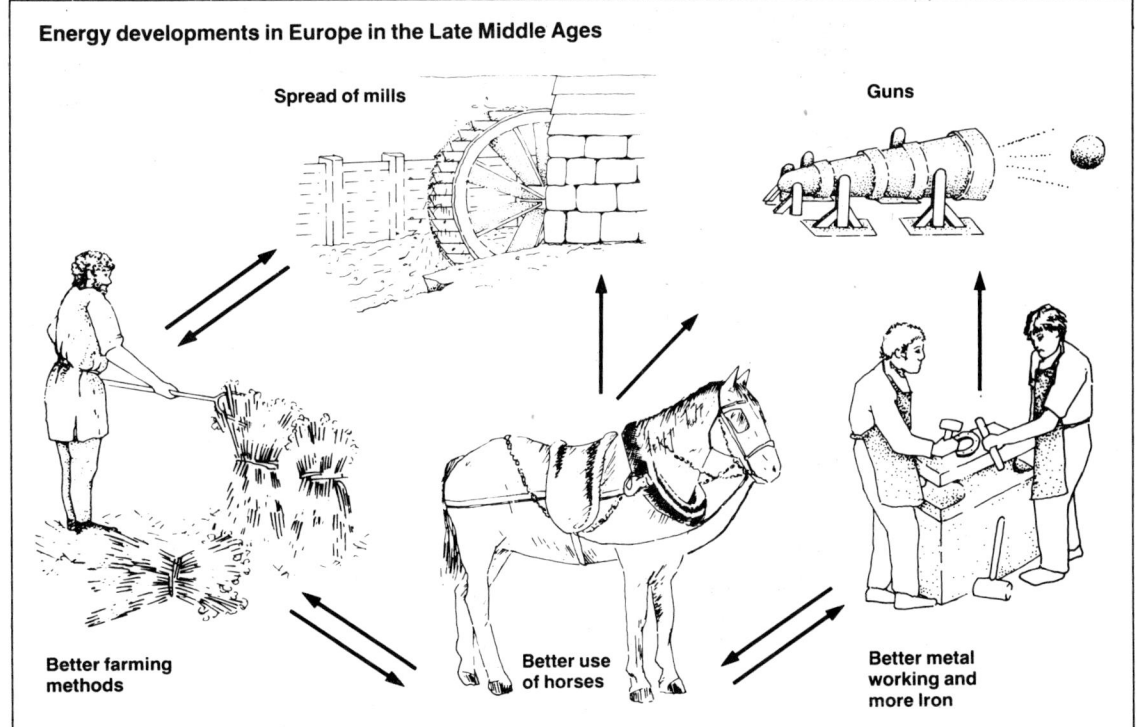

Energy developments in Europe in the Late Middle Ages

Spread of mills

Guns

Better farming methods

Better use of horses

Better metal working and more Iron

4: Speed of Change. The idea that change happens at uneven speeds, suggested as a discussion point here, is a general point of key importance. (See 'Speed of Change' pages 142–5)

5: Causation. The fact that the political and economic circumstances have to be right for a new technology to arise or to take root is one that is to be developed in 'Why Did it Happen then?' (pages 153–7). If in discussion of Medieval Europe pupils have seen that many factors, geographical, agricultural, technical and social combined to make for change, this will begin to build up the necessary conceptual framework to be consolidated later.

5: The second energy revolution to about AD 1800
pages 36–39

A: Objectives

After having used this section pupils should know that:
a) In the years 1500–1800 Europeans used well-established energy techniques to their limit.
b) This gave Europe the power to build up worldwide trade and Empire
c) This led, especially in Britain, to a wood shortage and to a change to coal.
d) In turn this led to such problems as air pollution, problems in industry (e.g. how to use coal for making iron) and pumping problems in the mines
e) The pumping problem led to the invention of the steam pump by Newcomen and others.
f) Watt, by inventing the rotatory steam engine in 1782 made a new prime mover, which by 1800 was being applied to drive machines of many sorts.

B: Discussion points

1: Why were the Europeans able to conquer much of the rest of the world in this period?

2: What were the disadvantages of the switch from wood to coal? (Either those percieved at the time, or those only apparent later. Pollution? reliance on exhaustible fossil sources of energy?)

3: What were the advantages? (Massively concentrated energy resource could be tapped. See diagram 'energy to drive machines' on page 149)

4: Why were a) Newcomen's steam pump b) Watt's rotative engine so important? In what ways was each different from all earlier prime movers? (They were both heat engines, using fire to do the work previously done by a horse etc. See also C4 below for comment)

5: Why did Britain take the lead in these developments? (see 'Why did it happen then? pages 153–7)

C: Difficulties and further information

1: The developments in this section represent a rather complex linkage of cause and effect. A diagram (see Figure E) may help some pupils to disentangle the links.

2: As the narrative approaches the present, evidence is much more plentiful, the pace of change more rapid and the worldwide connections more important. It becomes more difficult therefore to keep the main story-line clear. Teachers should beware of taking up too

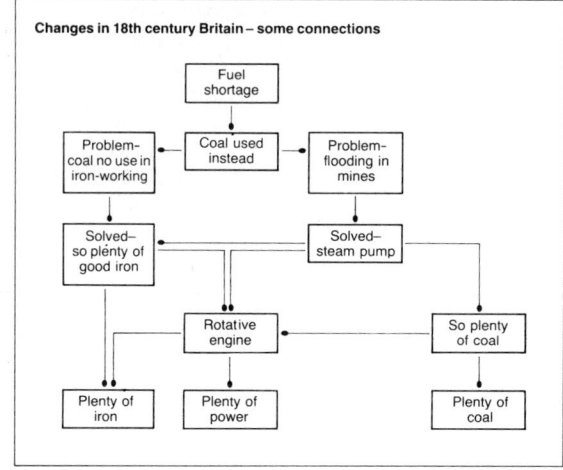

Changes in 18th century Britain – some connections

Figure E

many links with factors and problems in the narrative stage, and should skip with agility and determination.

3: The 'which caused which' problem raised on page 46 may be difficult for pupils who think that causes and effects in history are different sorts of animals, and who don't realise that a development like the steam engine can be both a cause and an effect at the same time.

4: The importance of the rotative steam engine is that it made it possible to turn heat energy into mechanical power of all kinds. Since there was a very large fossil store of heat energy readily accessible, this made the 'Second Energy Revolution' possible. Those pupils who know something about the physics involved will find this a simple idea, but it will be difficult for pupils who don't. However the idea that the steam engine tapped massive fuel supplies and coould turn them into useful work is very important, and can also be expressed in non-scientific terms. Some discussion of it at this stage will help pupils to see later that energy can be changed from one form into another, say into electrical energy, an important ingredient in seeing that there is a single 'world energy problem'.

5: In the interests of simplicity the narrative does not deal with the use of Newcomen engines for purposes other than pumping. They were in fact used to drive other machinery by pumping water over water wheels. Teachers who want to avoid the over-simplification might find the following source useful. (See also picture on page 162)

Mrs Darby Explains

'One of the consequences of the prosperity of my husband's works was that as they got very short of water in the summer of dry seasons they were obliged to blow very slow, and generally blow out the furnaces once a year, which was attended with very great loss. But my husband proposed the erecting of a Fire Engine to draw up the water from the lower works and convey it back to the upper pools, so that by continuous rotation of the water the furnace might be plentifully supplied. This answered exceedingly well, and others have followed the example.

(Letter from Abiah Darby, widow of Abraham Darby II, the Coalbrookdale Iron-master. Written about 1775)

6: How did it work? Non-technical teachers and pupils will find problems in understanding the working of the various steam engines. This is not at this stage necessary. It only becomes so in order to explain the role of Newcomen or Watt (See pages 153–7, or the role of science (See pages 136–8) in these changes. In science most pupils will already have been shown some more or less dramatic demonstrations of atmospheric pressure, and this might be recalled (or repeated). If a real explanation of 'how it worked' is to be attempted it should be done with models or using the drawings on page 138.

7: Capital. Some understanding of the idea of investment by partnerships and companies is needed to follow the narrative in the nineteenth and twentieth centuries. The word 'capital' is used in one of the boxes on page 45, and the idea of investment has already been raised in connection with water mills. Pupils should already have some ideas of the meaning of words like 'profit', 'interest', 'investment'. It would be useful to discuss these terms, and to explain the word 'capital' at this stage. Material designed to help to develop this more fully will be found in 'Government' pages 122–9 and in the material on Matthew Boulton on pages 161–4

D: Activities

Dramatised discussion of a plan to put a steam pump into a coal mine c. 1730.

Mine owner. 'Fire Engine' will cost over £1200 to build, and will need skilled men to repair it. Unreliable and new-fangled. (Teachers' role? Chairs and organises the discussion. The protagonists of the new machine should win. Owner might be old-fashioned and ultra-cautious type).

His son. Problems of existing methods. (Source 77 page 43) Has seen Fire Engine working-excited by its power. Deeper mine would mean more coal. Present levels soon exhausted?

A miner. Deeper mines, more explosions and gas, harder work.

Miner's wife. Agrees – she carries the coal up to the surface.

Other miners; men, women, children. Varying

views. Better pumps – less danger of drowning. What happens to people in the pit when the steam pump breaks? More coal means more work in the future. Any other work would be better than that in the pit. etc. etc.

Rich merchant. Will lend the £1200 at 8 per cent for ten years. Mine owner will get his money back and much more.

Captain of coal-ship trading to London. Great need for coal there. Price bound to rise so need to expand.

Engine builder. Full of promises and claims of success.

E: Exercises

1: Draw a time chart of the changes in energy use in Britain 1600–1800.

2: Read Source 62 and look at Source 61 on page 38.
a) What advantages in control of energy did the Europeans have over the Mexicans?
b) Without these advantages might the Europeans success–
i) have happened just the same?
ii) have happened much more slowly?
iii) never have happened at all?
Explain your answer.

3: Look at the following list of energy techniques used in Europe c. 1800.

Human labour
Horses
Oxen
Wind power for ships and mills
Water power
Guns and gunpowder
Wood and charcoal
Coal
Steam engines.

a) Which were new developments in the years 1500–1700?
b) Which were available in Roman times?
c) Which were probably most important and least important in the amount of energy they produced in 1800 (page 37)?
d) Which was most important in the history of energy? Explain your choice.

4: The problem of water in the mines had faced the Romans long before it faced the Europeans.
a) In what way did the Romans solve the problem?
b) In what way did the Europeans of the period 1500–1800 solve it?
c) Why did people of the two periods tackle the same problem in such different ways?

F: Links with factors and problems

1: Transport was of key importance in the development of coal mining, and coal transport is dealt with in more detail in 'Transport' pages 97–107. The sources on page 39 bring out the importance of transport clearly.

2: Science. This period is a turning point between one in which science was of little help to the practical man and one in which he could do little without it. Savery's and Newcomen's engines were based on the use of atmospheric pressure, a new concept of 17th century science. Savery, who had some scientific pretensions, failed where Newcomen, the practical man, succeeded. James Watt, scientist and craftsman, could not have done what he did without his scientific knowledge. There is more material on this in 'Ideas' pages 136–9, but teachers may wish pupils to begin to see the importance of science as they first come to the steam engine.

3: Causation. The coming together of the complex web of factors which made the steam engine possible in 18th century Britain is the subject of the case study of causation 'Why Did it Happen Then?' (page 153–7). This develops many points raised in this part of the narrative.

4: Steam power in later periods. Some pupils will not appreciate the importance of steam today–the fact, for instance, that nuclear energy in the latest power station is used simply to boil water to drive a steam engine. It may be useful to make this point when the steam engine first appears.

6: The second energy revolution (The energy revolution and the industrial revolution)
pages 47–57

A: Objectives

After using this section pupils should:

1: know that
a) A factory system based on water-powered machinery developed in Britain in the 18th century.
b) From about 1800 Britain began to switch to steam power. This led to;
i) industrial towns with quite different living and working conditions.
ii) railways and steamships.
c) By 1875 these new techniques had spread to other coal-rich countries.
d) These high energy-using countries with their steamships, railways and guns gained control of much of the rest of the world.

2: Be aware that the coming of industrial societies based on coal fuel and steam power represent a transformation as great as that between hunting and agricultural societies.

3: Be aware that the dependence on non-renewable fossil fuels was another change of historic importance.

B: Discussion points

1: The distinction between fossil fuels and renewable (page 47) is likely to open the obvious question of exhaustion of world reserves.

2: Has anything else happened in history quite so important as the neolithic and industrial revolutions? (Control of fire?)

3: Did the industrial revolution in Britain make life better or worse?

4: Why did these changes spread so rapidly and why to some countries and not to others? What did a country need to have first? (coal? iron? 'mechanically minded' people? good 'natural' communications?)

C: Difficulties and further information

1: As with the last section the story is very complex and teachers should be selective. Some confusion may in particular be caused by the fact that the industrial revolution was not at first powered by the new technology of steam, but by water power. Although untidy, this is an important point – change in history comes out of existing conditions and not out of the blue.

2: Teachers wishing to quantify the British switch to a coal-using economy may find the graph on page 105 useful. Figure F provides additional information.

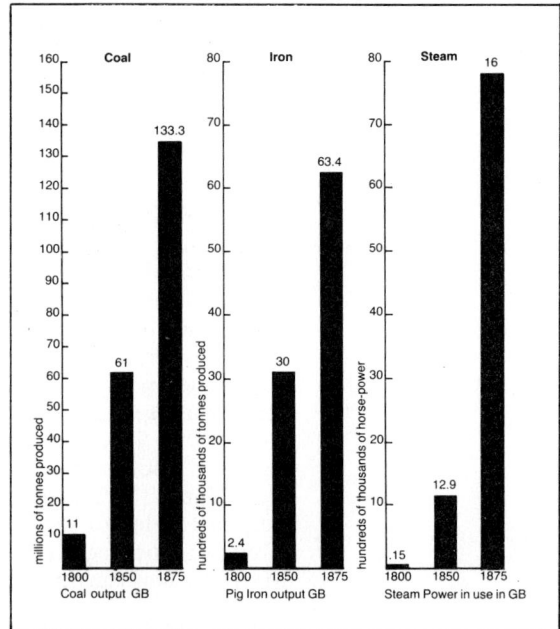

Figure F

3: The world-wide geographical spread may cause problems to those not sure where China is. There is world map featuring 19th century transport developments in 'Transport' page 105.

4: There is a considerable danger of the study of energy through time encouraging a narrowly technological interpretation of history. There is little time in this narrative to develop the economic, social and cultural factors that were essential ingredients in changes like the industrial revolution. This can to a some extent be corrected in dealing later with problems and factors, but in discussion e.g. of points B2 and 3 above, teachers may find opportunities to suggest that technology is only part of history.

D: **Activities**

1: Visits to museums or industrial sites or local studies. The changes dealt with in this and in the last section transformed most British towns and many rural areas too. Local sites are not likely to help with overview, but they will provide illustrative detail. Work done or to be done in a 'History Around Us' study might provide evidence of the growth of a town, the date of a gas-works, the opening of new collieries or railways etc.

2: Simulation game based on problem of installing steam power instead of or addition to water power in a textile mill, c. 1830. Players might represent rival mills, engineers, merchants, bankers. Play could be designed so that installing steam means regularity of production and capacity to expand. Resulting falling prices should squeeze water-powered mills.

E: **Exercises**

1: Look at Sources 82 and 83, page 48
a) What sources of energy can be seen?
b) What other sources of energy would be needed to make the things shown in the pictures?
c) When was each of these sources of energy developed or invented?
d) Which of them was most important to the people at the time? Why?
e) Which is most important in the history of energy? Why?

2: Make a list of the sorts of energy you have used in the last week (or year). Assume that the electricity you used was made in a coal-fired power station. (or teachers may wish pupils to discuss this point) Against each sort of energy write 'Renewable' or 'fossil'. Underline any that you might have used if you had lived in the 18th (or the 15th) century.

3: Coal and steam power made great changes in the 19th century.
a) What effect did they have on (i) where people worked (ii) the sort of work they did?
b) Did they make working conditions better or worse? In what ways?
c) Did they make living conditions better or worse? In what ways?
d) What effect did they have on i) world transport and ii) world trade?
e) What effect did they have on the power of Europe?

4: (Unguided version of 3 for able pupils) In what ways did the use of coal and steam power change the world in the 19th century?

5: The factory system began in the British cotton industry using the old-established energy of water power, and using animal power and wind power for transport. Does that mean that the industrial revolution would have happened just the same even without the steam engine?

6: (Using 'Tomorrow's World' page 55)
a) What conclusions might be drawn from this evidence about the attitude of the people of the time to the new source of power?
b) Today many people are opposed to energy changes like nuclear power. What evidence is there in pages 47–55 of people in early 19th century Britain opposing new forms of energy?

7: Read the following source and also source on page 53.

Steam engines make people behave better.

'The introduction of steam power and first class machinery necessitated great regularity of habit. This forced sobriety, and each succeeding generation has shown evidence of a population improving in habits of regularity, in physical strength, self-reliance and independence. . . I place great strength on the force of regular habits, and in no one thing has the system of mill-working done so much good as in the necessity it has compelled for regular attendance and habits. The capitalist will not put up the mill to have it unworked. If his engine moves he must have the hands follow the process. You cannot have regularity without sobriety and morality.'
E Potter, *View of a Manufacturing District, Glossop* '1856. Potter was a successful millowner.
a) Compare this evidence with that in the list of rules. Do these two sources contradict each other?
b) Potter was a millowner. Would a millworker of the time have been likely to agree with him about the advantages of steam? Explain your answer.

F: **Links with factors and problems**

1: Transport. It is in this period that steam made possible the building up of a world economic unit. There was not as yet a real world market in energy, because coal was so bulky although since it was almost essential as a fuel for ships and railways small amounts of it were carried to the ends of the earth for bunkering. The world energy market had to await the age of oil. These points are taken up in '*Transport*' pages 97–107.

2: War. Obvious links page 51. The 'Nemesis' incident is particularly useful in view of China's earlier technological lead, Britain's tiny comparative size, and the late 20th century position of Hong Kong. It demonstrates with great impact what coal and iron meant in terms of military power. Bismarck's famous reference to 'Blood and Iron' was not technologically very well-informed.

3: Speed of change. The rapidity of change in this period might be brought out by Exercise 2 above or in other ways, and comparisons with earlier periods encouraged in preparation of work on this problem.

4: Turning Points. The steam engine, the move to a coal-based economy, the reliance on fossil fuels, the industrial revolution, and the coming of a world economy are all good candidates for later discussion under this heading.

7: High energy civilisation. New sorts of energy and their impact
pages 57–81

A: Objectives
After using this section pupils should:

1: Know that (a) during the years since 1875 **three 'new' forms of energy have been exploited** –
i) Electricity, a method of transmitting energy, at first over short distances and in small amounts, but later for long distances in massive amounts.
   Electricity was made using the old technologies of steam and water power greatly developed by the turbine.
ii) Oil and natural gas. This made possible the motor car and the aeroplane powered by a new prime mover the internal combustion engine. It also made possible a world trade in energy.
iii) Nuclear Energy, first for war in the 1940s later for peaceful uses.

b) These new forms of energy have transformed industry and everyday life in the high energy countries.

2: Be aware of the enormous scale in the increase of energy use in this period and of the explosive rate of increase since 1945.

3: Be aware of the role of scientific knowledge in bringing about these new technologies.

B: Discussion points

1: Why were the i) electrical ii) oil/gas iii) nuclear inventions made at that time and place and not others?

2: What was the main advantge of i) electricity ii) oil/gas iii) nuclear energy over other forms of energy?
3: Tom Mullins (source 143 page 78) and Margaret Powell (source 144 page 79) lived in a world where steam power was well established. What difference had it made to their everyday lives?

4: What differences have i) electricity ii) oil/gas iii) nuclear energy made to everyday life?

5: Why was there a particularly rapid increase in energy use since 1945?

C: Difficulties

1: Again the main problem is with the amount of information. The narrative is the natural place for explanatory detail or linking items which may be useful in later work and with some pupils. *Teachers should use only what they need for the purpose in hand.*

2: The three 'new' forms of energy are dealt with in consecutive sub-sections which describe parallel periods of time. A fourth sub-section 'patterns of change' (pages 103–9) then discusses the changes as a whole. This may confuse pupils who expect events described on a later page to be subsequent to those on an earlier page. A time chart with three columns is a useful way of both overcoming this difficulty and recording the main points.

3: Technical knowledge.
a) A/C-D/C – Some understanding of the advantages of alternating over direct current is needed to see why electricity developed as it did. Clearly those who have some knowledge of the physics involved will find this easier than those who have none. But the fact that A/C could easily be transmitted over long distances is all that really matters, and discussion of electrons and their antics is only likely to confuse.
b) The internal combustion engine. The name implies technical knowledge, and may frighten some. But it is the only convenient name for these engines, perhaps the key prime movers of the 20th century. So it has to be used. The diagram on page 70 makes the basic point.

D: Activities

1: Models, or help from teachers of science or technology may be useful in getting technical ideas across. The basic ideas of a generator and an electric motor (page 58) can be demonstrated very simply with a bicycle with dynamo lighting and a battery powered toy. There is no need to know how either of these work.

2: Visits. Museum visits may help to explain technical points, but can also bemuse the non-technical with endless vistas of incredible machines. See 'Health warning' on page 52 of this guide. A visit to a power station may giuve a useful sense of scale. Some power stations and some parts of the grid system make a massive visual impact on the landscape which a teacher may be able to use.

3: There is a wealth of visual aid material available from the PR departments of the energy industry. See lists on page 53.

4: Collection of information from parents, grandparents etc. A class working on the impact of energy on everyday life in the 20th century could prepare lists (domestic uses e.g. electric light, non-domestic e.g. motor vehicles, work-related e.g. electric tools.) They might then collect a sample of local information from two generations to compare with the graphs on page 79, or with their own contemporary experience. This work might be used to give impact to the point that our familiar high energy everyday world is not very old.

E: Exercises

1: Compile a time chart of the main changes in this period.

2: Look back at the picture of a modern home on page 7.
a) List the energy sources shown in this picture, or needed to make the things shown.

b) Against each write the date at which i) it was first invented and ii) it came into widespread use (see activity 3 above).
c) 'By . . . . . . the new forms of energy had completely changed life in the home in Britain. Choose a date to fill the gap and explain your choice.

3: Choose one of
a) Electricity
b) Oil
c) Nuclear energy
and explain how and when it affected i) industry ii) ordinary life outside the home.

4: Look at Sources 103 and 107 pages 58 and 59.
If there were no captions or explanations with these sources, you could still tell from the sources themselves that they came from about the same date. How? (Both assume electric light was a novelty.)

5: (See Figure 5G) Cars like this were first made in Europe and N. America, in the period after 1885. Why could they not have been made earlier or elsewhere?

6: Look at Source 110 page 63.
a) What message did the artist who drew this advertisement want to give?
b) What can you tell from this source about peoples' attitudes to domestic machines at the time?

c) How could these attitudes be explained?

7: Look at the graph on page 81.
a) 'The 'Age of Coal' gave way to the 'Age of Oil' in . . . . .' Choose a date to fill the gap.
b) Explain your choice.
c) Why did this change-over take place?

8: Science and the new forms of energy.
a) In what way did scientific knowledge help in the development of electrical energy (or oil or nuclear).
b) Was science i) a slight help only or ii) a lot of help or iii) essential before electrical energy could be developed. Explain your choice.

F: **Links with factors and problems**

1: The material on the New York power cut (page 79) and much else in this section exemplifies the way people become dependent on new technological advance, as with the use of fire or the move to a farming economy at earlier periods. This may be related to the idea of progress. (See also next section on world energy problem. Have we gone down a technological blind alley?).

2: The galloping pace of change during this period makes an obvious contrast with earlier times, a point taken up under 'Speed of Change' (pages 142–5).

3: It is in this period that the area from which fuel can be carried, widening step by step since the

Figure G

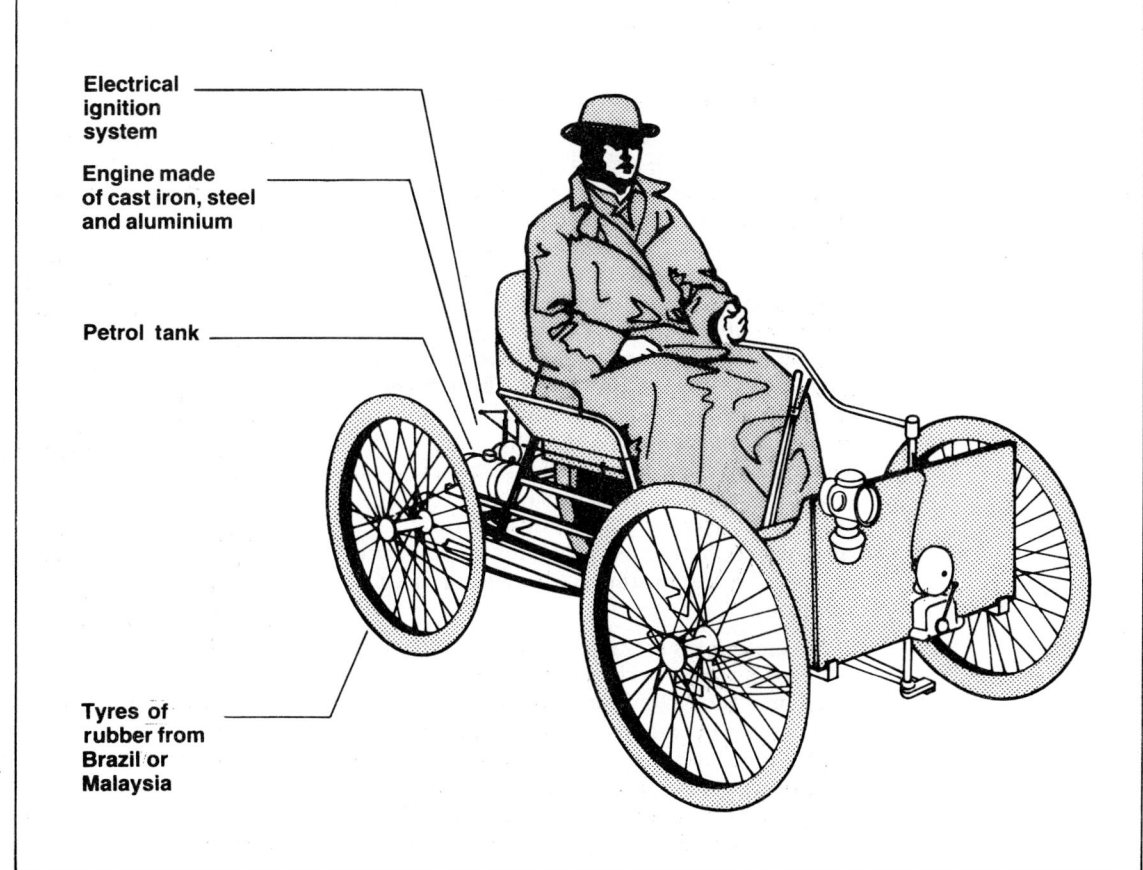

Electrical ignition system

Engine made of cast iron, steel and aluminium

Petrol tank

Tyres of rubber from Brazil or Malaysia

neolithic period, becomes the whole world area. See 'Transport' (pages 97–107).

4: The role of Government, which has been relatively unimportant in the 19th century, begins to be greater. There is fuller evidence of this in the next section and also in 'Government' (pages 122–30).

5: See 'War' (pages 90–6) for more material on the relationship of warlike and peaceful uses of nuclear energy.

6: Science is of such key importance in explaining electricity and nuclear energy, that it is treated here in the narrative. The 'Science' factor adds little to the material presented here.

8: High energy civilisation (Problems of high energy civilisation)
pages 82–89

A: **Objectives**

After using this section pupils should:

1: Know of the existence of serious problems
a) Fears of a world shortage of fossil fuels, especially oil.
b) Pollution
c) Political control of energy resources
d) Shortages of energy in the poor countries

2: Be aware that the most serious of these problems in human terms is that of the poor countries.

B: **Discussion points**

1: Are these problems similar to those of earlier periods?

2: Would earlier answers be likely to work now?

3: What new solutions might there be?

4: Could we go back to a low energy way of life?

5: Are the low energy countries likely to follow the same pattern of movement towards high energy technologies as have been followed by the rich countries in the past? Could this possibly happen, given the fears of a world energy shortage?

C: **Difficulties and further information**

1: The main difficulty is that the problems dealt with in this section are matters of current controversy. This means that many complex ideas and arguments are being propounded in public discussion, and teachers are not in a position to select those that matter most as they can when they are able to use the historian's hindsight. It also means handling issues like nuclear power, pollution and other hot potatoes in which passions are involved. These features are really an excellent opportunity to show that history is relevant to the contemporary world. The difficulty can be avoided if teachers remember the limited nature of the objectives – to start pupils thinking for themselves about these problems in a historical perspective, not to arbitrate between possible solutions.

2: No material is included on one pollution effect which is relevant to the world energy problem – the 'greenhouse effect' resulting from the increase in carbon dioxide in the atmosphere. This is omitted because it requires a good deal of technical explanation, and because it is not yet of any historical importance. But a balanced consideration of energy policy certainly requires it to be taken into account. Teachers attempting this may find this source useful. (Figure H.). For a discussion of the greenhouse and other global heating effects of high energy use see P Chapman op. cit. Chapter 6.

3: Pupils are not likely to know much about the geography of the Middle East or about political events there in the 1970s. Only a minimal knowledge is required, but teachers with very weak groups might choose to skip the text on pages 84–5, and rely on the map and the cartoon on page 85. The train of economic cause and effect shown in this is also complex, but discussion should help most pupils to make sense of it. It over-simplifies by implying that rising fuel prices were the only cause of rising prices.

D: **Activities**

1: The media carry a great deal about pollution, fuel prices and the politics of energy, from hypothermia among the poor to the building of Sizewell. A class at this stage of the work (or over a longer period) might collect cuttings, headlines and pictures for a wall newspaper. Items might be highlighted or simplified by the teacher, and sorted and discussed in relation to the work on 'problems'.

2: Class debate after discussion and preparation. 'We should aim to return to a simpler life using less energy.' or 'History shows that people can solve problems. So they will be able to solve the world energy problem without having to go back to a simple life.'

3: Groups of pupils represent: a) countries rich in oil. Saudi? b) industrial countries with little oil. Japan? c) poor countries. Bangladesh? d) Britain? e) animals?
   Groups discuss world energy policy with the following options:
a) Go on producing oil and natural gas fast as possible for as long as possible.
b) Limit oil production so as to make it last and keep the price high.
c) Encourage nuclear power stations and pay for them to be built in the poorest countries.
d) Forbid the building of nuclear power stations and close down the existing ones gradually.
e) Build many more hydro-electric power stations.
f) Research into other renewable sources of energy.
g) Stop closing down coal mines
h) Close down the coal mines which don't pay.
   When groups have decided on their policy, the class discusses the issues.

A hot time ahead for Planet Earth

Washington:. . . A potentially catastrophic warming of the earth will start in the 1990s, disrupting food production and raising coastal waters as the Polar icecaps melt, the Federal Government said in a report released yesterday.

The study, by the Environmental Protection Agency, said the climatic changes from the "greenhouse effect" are unavoidable, and warned, that the United States and other countries must begin searching for ways to mitigate the result.

The report concluded that even drastic and unlikely a step as a total ban on coal burning would delay by only 15 years a 3.6 degrees fahrenheit increase in average worldwide temperatures.

While other government studies have warned that the greenhouse effect was a potential problem, the new report is the first to state with certainty that the warming will occur no matter what is tried to restrict the use of fossil fuels.

The study is based on early projections by the National Academy of Sciences that a doubling of carbon dioxide in the air – which could occur by the middle of the next century – would raise present world temperatures within a range of 2.7 degrees fahrenheit (1.5)c to 8.1 degrees.

This result is known as the greenhouse effect because the carbon dioxide acts like the glass in a greenhouse, allowing the sun's warming rays to reach earth but not allowing the heat to escape. The study called for a sense of urgency in planning how to deal with the coming temperature changes.

"Temperature increases are likely to be accompanied by dramatic changes in precipitation and storm patterns and a rise in global average sea level. As a result, agricultural conditions will be significantly altered, environmental and economic systems potentially disrupted and political institutions stressed." the study warned – AP.

E: Exercises

1: Imagine that the diagram on page 86 (Who buys the world's energy supplies?) was a cartoon with speech bubbles. Write speeches for the bubbles.

2: Examine the sources on page 83 (pollution newspaper cuttings) These are all secondary sources.
a) Where possible say what primary sources each used.
b) How reliable were these primary sources likely to be?
c) Is there evidence that any of the journalists cross-checked with other primary sources?
d) Had the journalists any reason to distort the news?
e) Which source seems most reliable? Explain why.

3: You are managing director of an oil company in 1974, just after the first big rise in oil prices. (i) Choose one of these policies:
a) Put up the price of petrol and other products to match. This way you can go on making as much profit as before.
b) Put up prices to some extent, but also cut profits to some extent.
c) Put up prices as little as you can, cutting profits almost to nothing.
(ii) Now choose one of these policies:
x) Spend as much as possible prospecting for new oil-fields.
y) Invest as much of the company's money as possible in wind-powered generators and solar power.
z) Don't invest any money in anything. (iii) Explain your choice of policies to the shareholders of the company.

4: Read source 152 page 86.
a) In what ways is the problem faced by these women the same as that faced in the New Stone Age (pages 12–15)?
b) In what ways is it different?

F: Links with factors and problems

1: The world energy problem and various suggested ways of solving it are examined more fully in 'Shortage and Conservation' pages 116–21.

2: The problems of the high energy civilisation do much to explain the increased government influence and control of energy which has taken place in the 20th century. See 'Government and Energy' pages 126–29.

3: The energy plight of the third world countries is clearly relevant to the idea of progress. Progress for whom? Many pupils may have the notion suggested as a basis for discussion in B5 above, that it is only a matter of time before the whole world 'catches up' with an affluent norm. The fact that this is in energy terms so improbable as to verge on the impossible is clearly food for thought.

4: Turning Points. The point (1973?) when it became clear to policy makers that the fossil fuel resources of the earth are finite is clearly a turning point of some magnitude. Its magnitude will be even greater if the suggested alternatives such as nuclear energy should also soon find their limits.

5: In 'Speed of Change' pupils are invited to look for examples of 'Dead Ends'. Is oil-fired central heating likely to last as long as the hypocaust? (see page 145) 'Speed of Change' also discusses intermittent changes which stop and then re-start. It takes solar heating as an example. Some knowledge of the world oil problem is needed to make sense of this.

5: Revision and assessment, 1

When the rapid narrative overview (stage 1 in the suggested strategy) has been completed, a short period of revision will help to consolidate knowledge, and an assessment will enable the teacher to see what assumptions can be made in stage 2, or what remedial action needs to be taken first.

Summaries are provided within 'Energy Through Time' to help with this revision:
page 16   8000 to 3500 BC
page 28   3500 to 500 BC
page 35   500 BC to AD 1500
page 56   1500 to 1875
page 87   Since 1875

These summaries might be used as the basis of a class or group discussion to produce a single brief summary of the whole narrative.

The following exercises might be used as revision work or for assessment.

1: One important feature of the history of energy has been the development in turn of a series of prime movers. Make a list of these in the order in which they became important, and against each write the approximate date, place of first use or invention, and the name of any known inventor.

Or: (a 'stepped' version of the same exercise, which makes greater conceptual demands but looks much simpler because less literary)
Look at the following list:
Internal combustion engines
Water-mills
Steam engines
Windmills
Animal power

a) Write a heading for the list
b) Place the list in correct order of historical development and give an approximate date to each
c) Choose one pair of items in the list which *could not* be in a different order. Explain your choice.

2: During the history of energy various sources of energy have become important. Make a list of these in the order in which they became important, and against each write the .

approximate date, place where the development took place, and name of any known inventor.

3: The items in the following list A each helped to cause an item in list B.

List A:
1: Farming developed in the Middle East.
2: River and sea-going ships were invented in Egypt and elsewhere.
3: There were many water-mills in Europe in the later Middle Ages.
4: There was a wood shortage in 17th. century in Britain.
5: Oil was cheap and plentiful by the year 1900.

List B
a) Large cities became possible.
b) Iron production was able to increase.
c) Aeroplanes could be developed.
d) The steam engine was developed.
e) Fuel was needed for new purposes.

a) Write down the number and letter of the items from lists A and B which go together.
b) Write a sentence or so explaining how each list A item helped to cause its list B item.
(This could be made easier by not jumbling the order of list B, or harder by adding other items)

Or: Write a paragraph on how each of the following affected the history of energy, giving *dates*, *places* and *effects*.
a) The development of farming
b) The development of cities and civilisation
c) The Industrial Revolution

4: The following lists show in a jumbled order some of the prime movers that have been developed at various times and some of the needs for energy that have been important.

List A: Prime movers
a) Water-mills
b) Animals to turn machines
c) Internal Combustion Engines
d) Steam Engines
e) Windmills

List B: Energy needs
1. To pull war chariots
2. To transport fuel
3. To make iron
4. To make pottery
5. To make electricity
6. To drive machines in factories
7. To drive mills to grind corn
8. To pull ploughs
9. To cook food

Against each of the following write the letter(s) from list A and the number(s) from list B which would be in use at that time and place:

Europe in the Old Stone Age.
Palestine in the New Stone Age
Egypt c 1000 BC
Rome c AD 10
China c AD 200
Europe c AD 1500
Britain c AD 1900

5: Explain briefly the meaning of each of the following words and where appropriate give an example from the history of energy

Nomad
Threshing
Yoke
Civilisation
Prime mover
Pollution
Fossil fuel
Internal combustion engine
Hydro electricity
Radio-active

6: Choose the *one* of the following developments which was most important in the history of energy: The use of fire; the development of iron working; the use of water power; the steam engine; oil; electricity.
   Give reasons for your choice.

7: World map with letters as follows

A. Mesopotamia   B. Egypt   C. India
D. China   E. Britain   F. Europe
G. N America   H. Palestine.

The following list gives the dates at which various countries or regions led the world in energy technology.
   (i) Against each date write the letter of the region which was in the lead at that time.

6000 BC (H)
3500 BC (A)
1000 BC (B)
AD 800 (D)
AD 1500 (F)
AD 1800 (E)
AD 1980 (G?)

ii) Choose *one* (?) of these and give reasons for your choice.

8: Look at the following list of energy resources available at different times.

   1. Good supply of oxen with effective harness.
   2. Good supply of horses with effective harness.
   3. Water mills.
   4. Wind mills.
   5. Reliable rainfall most of the year.
   6. Frequent winds.
   7. Extensive forests for fuel supply
   8. Ships capable of crossing the oceans.
   9. Guns.
   10. Many skilled craftsmen e.g. millwrights
   11. Good supply of coal for fuel
   12. Good supply of oil for fuel

a) Against the following countries write the numbers from the list of the resources which were important there at the date given:

Egypt 1000 BC
Rome AD 100
China AD 400
Britain AD 1700
USA AD 1900

b) Choose *one* of these countries and dates. Which was its most important energy resource at that time? Give reasons for your choice.
c) Choose the energy resource which has been most the important taking the whole history of energy into account. Explain why you chose it.

6: Teaching the factors

Introduction

A: Objectives
After having studied the operation of two or more factors pupils should be able to:
1: Grasp the story-line of the narrative more fully and recall its details more clearly.
2: Understand the importance of continuity in history, that some things have stayed in some ways the same for very long periods, and that similar influences have been present at many periods.
3: Use the term 'factor' effectively in history, and demonstrate how a single causative influence operated.
4: Understand that to explain historical events the combination of several factors must be studied.

B: Some general strategies

1: The text and cartoon on page 89 aim to warn against an over-simple idea of how factors operate in history. The factors chosen by the author are only one possible group. The class might begin its work on factors by discussing what have been the important influences on the history of energy use in addition to those suggested on page 89. Other broad factors like agriculture or industry might be suggested, or more precise and concrete ones such as the horse or the development of metal-working. Others might be the skill of craftsmen, the need to save labour and avoid effort, or the activities of business-men and capitalists.

At this opening stage when misconceptions might be formed teachers may be able to use the cartoon to suggest that factors are selected for convenience of study by the historian and do not appear in the record conveniently labelled as factors. Alternatively teachers may wish to come back to the rather abstract ideas on page 89 after one or two actual factors have been studied.

2: Teachers may decide to set work on one of the alternative factors suggested above, or to set able pupils to work for themselves on a factor of their own choice. Index entries will be found which could support the alternatives suggested above and others.

3: *A teacher should be ready to skip and select according to the purpose in hand.* For instance a central idea of the 'transport' factor is that transport has made fuels available from wider and wider radii, terminating in the world market of the 20th century. With some groups this might be put across more clearly by a rapid use of one or two maps and sources than by working through the whole of pages 97–107.

4: Teachers may wish to use alternative material of their own. For instance the 'ideas' factor omits all reference to the difficult but important scientific developments in the 19th century in the concept of energy itself. A teacher with an able group of pupils who know some physics may wish to include further material. See discussion below, page 35.

5: Since a leading purpose of the study of factors is to consolidate overview, the class might start work on each factor with a discussion of what is known already from the narrative about occasions when it was important (or was notable by its absence), or how its influence operated.

6: The introduction to each factor poses one or more leading questions. The material which then follows has been selected so as to help pupils to answer these. But many of these leading questions may be answered, at least tenatatively, by reference to the narrative alone. Discussion of such answers might form a route into a factor.

Factors 1: War
pages 89–96

A: **Objectives**

After using this chapter pupils should have advanced towards the objectives on page 31 above and should in particular be able to:

1: Explain how the development for warlike purposes of i) the horse, ii) guns iii) nuclear energy contributed to changes in the history of energy.
2: Understand that factors can operate indirectly through a chain of cause and effect, as in the series
war – guns – iron-founding – wood-shortage – coal use. (See diagram, page 95)
3: Recognise that war has in general operated to accelerate changes which were made possible or initiated by other factors.

B: **Difficulties**

1: Pupils are likely to confuse the effects of war on energy developments with the effects of energy developments on war. These last are immense, may well interest many pupils, and have great historical importance, but they should be avoided. In this study it is only necessary to recognise that events like the coming of guns or the dropping of the A bomb had importance, not to study this importance in detail. The study should be of how such events were caused by (or caused) changes in the history of energy.

2: The idea of a chain of causation is complex. A diagram may help some pupils to make the necessary connection (see page 95 and Diagram I below). A diagram of this type might be constructed in class discussion, used as an exercise (see Exercise 2 below) or used as a

method of recording an agreed version of the development.

3: The time chart on page 96, by setting out the evidence of date in isolation from other evidence about causal links may lead pupils into an over-simple view that the warlike uses of nuclear energy, since they came first, must have in a straightforward way 'led to' the peaceful uses. In fact the connection is more complex, and war acted as the forcing house of changes already in train in 1939. Exercises B and C below may help pupils to see this point.

4: Why guns in Europe and not in China? (page 94) A simple approach is suggested in the text, in terms of the political fragmentation of Europe. For a balanced discussion Chinese factors should also be considered, but this is not practicable. See discussion above p. 17

5: Some confusion may be caused by the inclusion of peaceful uses of the horse in this section. This is done because war was at any rate an important, and perhaps a necessary spur to the extensive use of horses, which were to be the main source of portable energy until the twentieth century.

C: **Activity**

A class discussion of the question, 'How important was war as a factor in the history of energy?' might be a useful way of summing up this topic.

1) The class makes a list of the most important developments or changes in the history of energy. (One such list might be: harnessing of fire, animals, water, wind, steam, oil, coal, uranium)
2) In groups pupils decide whether each of these

was directly or indirectly in an important sense affected by war.

3) The groups then each contribute to a whole class discussion of the main question.

(Note that an important conclusion might be that most important developments before the 20th century were only indirectly affected by war. Another might be that war was important as an accelerator of changes which were made possible by other factors, such as the growth of science.)

D: **Exercises**

1: Use the index heading 'Horses – war' to find all the pictures of the warlike use of horses.
a) List the improvements or inventions that can be seen in these pictures which helped to make the horse into a deadly weapon of war.
b) Choose one (or more?) of these improvements which was important. Explain where and when it developed and how it made the horse more effective in war.
c) Some of these improvements also made the horse more useful in peace. Write the letter 'P' against each of these in your list.
d) i) 'The warlike uses of the horse were less important in the history of energy than the peaceful uses.'
ii) 'The warlike uses of the horse were more important in the history of energy than the peaceful uses.'
iii) 'The warlike uses of the horse were of equal importance in the history of energy to the peaceful uses.'

Choose the one of these statements that you agree with and explain your choice.

See Figure I

2: In this diagram the arrows (or some of the arrows) showing that one item helped to cause another have been left out. Copy the diagram and draw in the arrows. Choose *two*(?) of them and explain in each case how one of the items they connect helped to cause the other.

3: Read source 133 (pages 74–5)
In his letter Einstein makes several suggestions about what might happen.
a) Which of these turned out as he suggested?
b) On which of these was he wrong?

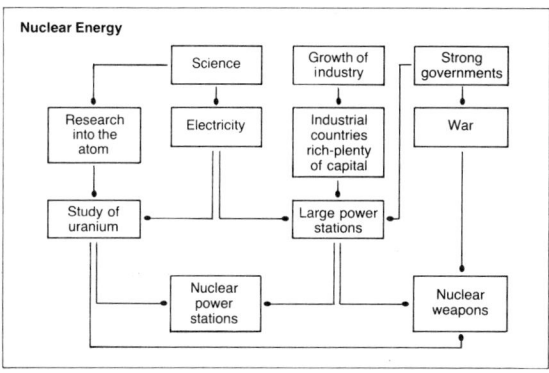

Figure I

c) Use the information on the diagram on page 75 to explain why the Manhattan Project could only have been carried out in a country like the USA.
d) What evidence is there in Einstein's letter that he thought nuclear energy might have peaceful as well as warlike uses?
e) What factors apart from war helped to make nuclear energy possible in the later 20th century?
f) What part did the war against Hitler play in bringing about peaceful uses of nuclear energy?

4: Look at Source 167 page 93
a) What advantage would a mill like this give to the army that owned it?
b) Would mills like this be likely to be of any peaceful use in Europe in 1606?
c) What other military uses of energy are shown in the picture as well as the horses turning the mill?
d) If the date of the picture was not given you could still work it out. What are the earliest and the latest possible dates for the picture?
e) Give reasons for your answers to part d).

5: The coming of horses, guns and nuclear power are all ways in which war affected the history of energy.
a) In what other ways did it do so? (Guidance suggestions could be included – metallurgy, ship-building, ic engine, use of oil. Pupils could be guided to index entries on these.)
b) Did war start new energy-using techniques or encourage those which were happening in any case?

Factors 2: Transport
page 97–107

A: **Objectives**

After using this chapter pupils should have advanced towards the objectives on page 31 above and should in particular be able to:

1: Outline the process of widening energy 'markets' from the neolothic village to the global village.
2: Explain in specific cases how transport changes were necessary conditions for developments in energy use. (See Exercises 3, 5, and 8 below)
3: Explain how these transport changes did not

act alone but in combination with other factors. (see Exercise 4 below)

B: **Difficulties**

1: Reference back to the narrative will of be needed. Pupils should by this stage know their way around it, and should be encouraged to use the index.

2: Problems of numeracy are likely to arise. This is not because of complexity – nothing beyond simple multiplication and division is needed. The difficulty may arise if pupils do not expect to calculate in a history lesson, and do not see its value. It is however the case that a precise numerical calculation can make a historical point much more convincingly than the use of vague superlatives. See exercise 3. below. If pupils can be brought to see the special force of a numerically precise argument, they will have learned something of value.

A kindred problem may arise with the use of approximations. Pupils may not be used to making approximations as they are invited to do in Exercise 1. But this is useful provided the approximations are based on evidence. The approximations of Exercise 1 should help pupils to see changes in the availability of fuel more effectively, thus bringing one of the clearest patterns of 'Energy Through Time' into sharp focus.

3: In some cases precise figures are available in the sources, so that the effect of transport costs on the cost of fuel or other goods can be seen. (e.g. S. 195 page 104) In earlier periods such figures are rare. But transport always had a cost, and this was at most periods a powerful limitation on the availability of fuel. Exercise B below is designed to help pupils to see this. The cartoon on page 107 might be used to sharpen their perception, since the cost of 'space mining' seems likely to make it little more that an artist's fantasy.

C: Activities

Simulation of a possible argument about the building of a canal in Britain c 1790. For many areas this could be in the region of the school.

Using pages 102–4, groups or individuals might prepare arguments from the point of view of:

1: Canal engineer
2: Land owner
3: Coal owner
4: Farmers
5: Townspeople, rich and poor.
6: Iron-master
7: Steam engine builder
8: Road carrier
9: River boatman

The class, led by the spokespersons for each group might then conduct the argument. If taped and played back this can lead to useful discussion in analysis of alleged errors or anachronisms.

D: Exercises

1: Complete the following table:
'Transport and Energy Through Time'
Columns
Period of history
Transport methods used
Types of energy used
Fuel carried how far (approx.)
Rows
Neolithic times 8000 to 3500 BC
Low energy civilisations to AD 500
Middle Ages
1500–1800

1800–1900
since 1900

2: Source 191 page 103 shows clearly what it cost to transport coal on the river Thames in 1738. At other periods of history we have no such figures. But even when people did not use money things could not be transported for nothing. People had to make things like boats, supply things like food, or do without things like useful work, to make any form of transport possible. Counting these things as 'costs', look at the following sources and decide what the costs were for:
The American farmer in Source 176 page 97
The African farmer in Source 177 page 97
Cato in Source 180 page 98
The boatmen in Source 186 page 100

3: Read Source 191 page 103 and Source 195 page 104
a) In 1738 coal cost 153 pence a cauldron in London. How much would it cost in Abingdon?
b) How much would this be per tonne?
c) How much did the people of Manchester pay per tonne before the building of the canal?
d) How much did they pay afterwards?
e) Why was the cost so much less at Manchester than at Abingdon even before the canal?
f) Use these calculations to explain why industry developed rapidly in the 18th century in Manchester, and not in Abingdon.

4: China had had good canal transport, and was also able to use coal to make iron at least 1000 years earlier than Britain. (See map page 17) But it was Britain in the 18th century that the second energy revolution began. Why did this happen in Britain and not in China?

5: Oil is much easier to transport than coal or wood.
a) Why is this? (see page 69)
b) What effect did this have on:
i) new engines
ii) new vehicles
iii) everyday life
iv) world trade.

6: Horses first became important for war rather than for transport. Today they are more important for leisure use. i) What were the main stages by which horses became important for transport? ii) What were the main stages by which they lost that importance?

7: **Advertisement**

Ashby de la Zouch intended canal. Cost of freight of a waggon load of coals to be delivered at the intended wharf at the above mentioned place at the rate of 2d. per ton per mile.

From Donisthorpe (1.5 miles) By canal 7½d (3p) by land 3s 6d (16.5p)

From Dudlington (20 miles) By canal 7s 1d (35p) by land 18s (90p)

(From the *Leicestershire Journal* 14 December 1792)

a) What was the advantage of this canal according to this source?

b) How reliable is the source as evidence of why canals were built in Britain at the time?
c) What other evidence is there to support this explanation of the canal building?

8. a) Choose *one* of the following and explain i) what transport changes helped to make it possible, ii) how they did so.

Iron working in Roman times
The increased use of coal in 18th century Britain.
The increased use of coal in 19th century Britain.
The growth of the oil industry since 1860.

b) What other changes apart from those in transport were needed to bring about the development you discussed in part a)?

Factors 3: shortage and conservation
pages 108–121

A: Objectives

After using this chapter pupils should have advanced towards the objectives on page 28 above and should in particular be able to:

1: Identify periods of history when shortages of energy have been of importance, and other when they have not.

2: Explain some of the main methods by which shortages have been tackled at different periods, including the conservation of existing sources and the development of new ones.

3: Show how shortage and conservation have encouraged or inhibited change or development at different periods.

4: Compare the twentieth century problem of rapidly expanding energy use and finite resources of fossil fuels with shortage problems of earlier periods.

B: Difficulties

1: The two periods when shortage of energy has had most impact have been dealt with in some detail in the narrative. Pupils will need to refer back to pages 39–49 for the effect of the wood shortage in 17/18th century Britain, and to pages 80–2 for the coming of the late 20th century world energy problem.

2: Pupils may have a simple idea of shortage as a matter of bare cupboards. In practice there has usually been fuel at a distance and at a price, so shortages have been acute for some people (usually the poor) and in some places, while for others they have been much less serious.

3: There is a kindred complexity in the idea of reserves of fuels (see graph on pages 118 and 119). These are reserves known to exist at a given date and economically exploitable with a given technology. For instance the very great rise in oil prices in the 1970s made exploration for and exploitation of arctic or deep off-shore oil economic, so known reserves are increasing and are likely to continue to do so, but at a declining rate and at increasing cost.

C: Activities

1: Collection and discussion of press-cutting and other media references. The world energy åroblem, the discovery of new reserves, and the development of new conservation methods are often in the news. So every winter is hypothermia amongst the old and poor.

2: A class activity leading to written exercise. To be done at the end of a period of work on this factor.

The class is divided into three groups:

1: Takes period before AD 1500 (pages 109–12)
2: Takes period 1500–1900 (pages 113–17)
3: Takes period 1900–present (pages 117–21)

Each group finds out and agrees its answers to three questions:
a) How serious a problem were shortages of energy for the people living at that time?
b) What did they do to try to solve the problem?
c) How important were shortages as a factor causing change or development?

Spokesperson for each group explains its findings to the class.

Written question for all – 'Choose two periods of history one when shortage was important in causing change, and one when it had little importance. Explain your choices.'

D: Exercises

1: Write down the following list of methods by which people have dealt with problems of energy shortage:
i) Doing without
ii) Fetching fuel from a distance
iii) Finding a new source of energy
iv) Conservation to avoid waste and use energy more efficiently
v) Government control of energy supplies.

a) Look through pages 108–21 write against each method the number of the source which shows it in use.
b) Refer back to the narrative and write against each method the number of any sources or pages of narrative which show that method in use.
c) Choose *one* of these methods. Explain with examples how and when it was used and say how important you consider it to have been in solving the problem.

2: (Alternative to 1)
a) Study pages 119–21 and list the methods of dealing with shortage that you find there.
b) Look at pages 108–18. Write against each method in your list the number of any sources which show it in use and the date to which the source applies.
c) Write an answer to the question, 'In what ways are modern methods of dealing with energy shortage similar to those used in the past. In what ways are they different?'

3: Sources 198 and the photograph on its left (page 108) show people living in a very primitive and uncivilised way, who appear to be happy.

Source 222 page 117 describes civilised people living in twentieth century Britain who appear to be miserable. Does this mean that the evidence is misleading? Explain your answer.

4: 'Problems of energy shortage have been solved in the past. This proves that the present world shortage can also be solved. Do you agree with this statement?

5: Sources 219 and 221 (pages 116–17) both made predictions about the future. Which of their predictions have proved right and which wrong in the time since they were written?

Factors 4: government and energy
pages 122–129

A: **Objectives**

After using this chapter pupils should have advanced towards the objectives on page 31 above and should in particular be able to:

1: Identify occasions when governments (or quasi-governmental authorities like lords of the manor) have influenced energy use.
2: Explain the actions taken by these bodies and discuss their effects.
3: Identify periods, especially the period of the industrial revolution in Britain, when major decisions were taken about energy developments with little government participation.
4: Describe and explain the important increases in government influence on energy developments in the twentieth century.

B: **Difficulties**

1: This chapter deals with less concrete ideas than war, transport and shortage. The text attempts to be as accessible as possible by using concrete terms like 'governments' or 'business men' instead of 'the state' or 'entrepeneurs', and some work can be done which keeps very near the concrete. However even the term 'government' is confusing to many pupils and teachers should bear in mind the need to clarify it as the work proceeds.

The issues connected with the role of the state and of private enterprise are complex and contentious. They are however, of the greatest importance and of central relevance to the history of energy in the 20th century. Young people of 16 need to understand as much as they can of the role of the multinationals or of the state. The aim of this chapter is not to arbitrate on the complex issues involved but to provide materials which can be used to start pupils thinking about them.

2: There is a great deal of overlap with other parts of the book, notably the narrative pages 84–5 and the 'factor' chapters on War (pages 90–96) and Shortage and Conservation (pages 107–122). Much of the material on Matthew Boulton (pages 161–4) or Thomas Edison (pages 165–7) might also be used in work on the role and attitude of the entrepeneur. The index entries on 'Government' and 'Capital' will be found useful. See Exercise 4 below for one suggestion.

C: **Activities**

1: As with Shortage and Conservation, media references to state controls or to the role of the multinationals in current oil politics and economics are frequent. A class might usefully collect and discuss press cuttings, partly as sources of information and partly as pieces of evidence to be evaluated.

2: The energy industry provides a great deal of information material some of it aimed at school children. So does the Department of Energy. So do pressure groups like the Friends of the Earth. (See addresses on page 50). A class might study material of this sort related to government policy and control or the need for it, and consider its reliability in relation to the interests of those who produced it.

3: Discussion of the merits of government controls of energy might be a useful way of summing up the work and encouraging further thought. Pupils are likely to have opinions based either on prejudice or on the work they have already done. Groups made up of those who had like opinions might be set to search for ammunition to support their views, using pages 122–9 and the index to guide them to other pages. Each group might then prepare arguments for a class discussion.

D: **Exercises**

1 a) Make a list (or use list agreed by the class) of the ten (?) most important developments in the history of energy, and the approximate date of each.
b) Against each item on your list write the letter 'G' if a government took an important part in bringing that development about.
c) What can you conclude from this? (Governments always important? Governments never important? Governments important at one time but not at others?)
d) What explanation can you suggest for your conclusions?

or 2: Governments have at different times taken action to control how people used energy or how they obtained it, with the following aims:
i) to prevent pollution
ii) to conserve scarce supplies
iii) to encourage new supplies
iv) to make sure of supplies for war
v) to stop other people controlling important sources of energy
a) Copy down this list and against each item write the number of any sources which are examples of this, and the date of the events to which the source refers.

b) Which reasons have been important only or mainly in the 20th century?

c) What explanation can you suggest for this?

3: The period since 1950 has been called the 'Age of Oil.' Explain why. Use Table 4 page 124, the graphs of world energy use on pages 80 and 81 and your background knowledge of the modern use of energy from oil in everyday life and work. (NB. Atlantic Richfield and ENI are also oil companies as well as the companies in table 4 who are obviously so.)

4: a) Explain why each of (or any two of?) the following people decided to spend money on new developments in energy.

i) The Abbot of Glastonbury (page 33)

ii) Matthew Boulton (Use index, but especially sources 289 page 157 and 299 page 162)

iii) Thomas Edison (use index but especially page 165)

iv) John D Rockefeller (use index)

b) Would the new developments have taken place without people prepared to spend money as they did?

5: Use the sources on slavery on page 122–3, and other information about slavery (see index entry) and also the following:

'Gangs of slaves should be formed, not exceeding ten men each. The work should be arranged so that the men will be working singly or in pairs, because they are difficult to guard when dispersed. For those who are in chains there should be a barracks, as healthy as possible, lit by a number of windows so high up that they cannot be reached with the hand.'
(Roman handbook of advice to farmers. Columella's 'Agriculture' c AD 50)

a) How did governments help to make slavery possible?

b) What disadvantages in the use of slavery or forced labour are shown in these sources?

c) Why, in spite of these disadvantages did slavery come into widespread use in the ancient civilisations?

d) In the nineteenth and twentieth centuries governments have passed laws forbidding slavery. This is partly because people had come to believe it was wrong. What other reason can you suggest?

Factors 5: ideas and the history of energy
pages 130–140

A: **Objectives**

After using this chapter pupils should have advanced towards the objectives of page 31 above and should in particular be able to:

1: Identify occasions on which a) religious thinking and b) scientific thinking have at different times contributed to continuities or to changes in the history of energy.

2: Explain how they did so.

3: Identify the development of the steam engine as the first energy change in which scientific knowledge played a necessary part, and explain what this part was.

4: Recognise that very ancient attitudes to fire retain some of their potency in the modern world, and see this as the sharing of a continuous experience by people of past and present.

B: **Difficulties**

1: As with other factors there is much overlap. In the period since the steam engine, developments like gas, electricity, oil and nuclear energy have all been based on a scientific foundation of increasing solidity, and therefore reference to the scientific factor has been a necessary part of the narrative. Pupils will often need to refer to material there. See index entry 'Science'.

2: Pupils will vary widely in the degree to which they understand the science involved. This is vital only at points where scientific knowledge is needed see why things happened in history. These points are:

a) Knowledge of atmospheric pressure is needed to understand the work of Papin, Savery and Newcomen.

b) Some knowledge of the physics of evaporation and condensation is needed to understand the separate condenser. Pupils familiar with the ideas of specific heat and latent heat, both worked out by Joseph Black, Watt's colleague, will be greatly advantaged. This can be short-circuited by a simple act of faith that the separate condenser was a great step forward in efficiency and was only likely to be developed by someone who understood these ideas. But if, perhaps with aid of colleagues in the science department, teachers can bring pupils to follow some of Watt's scientific thinking, the latter will know more history as well as more science.

c) Knowledge that oil and gas are complex chemicals which need to be refined in order to be used for various purposes is needed to understand the development of these two fuels. Actual knowledge of the chemistry involved is not important.

d) Knowledge about electricity is needed to understand its early development, but only at a basic level, such as that it flows along wires or other conductors and can make them glow. Pupils familiar with the principles on which generators and electric motors work will feel more at home with their history but that will be their main advantage.

e) Knowledge of the physics of alternating currents and of transformers will help pupils to understand the 'Battle of the Systems' between Edison and Tesla. Those who understand Ohm's law will see easily how very high voltages make possible efficient transmission. But it is not necessary to understand these matters to see the advantages of a.c.

f) Knowledge that nuclear physics uses electrical techniques in research is needed explain why it began when it did, but more detailed knowledge is likely to be helpful rather than essential. Those who feel the numerical force of Einstein's famous equation will find it easier to understand subsequent developments; those who know what chain reactions are will understand better the difficulty of starting them in bombs and controlling them in reactors; those who have learned about radio-activity will understand better the problems of nuclear pollution. But the outline history of all these matters can be followed without scientific detail.

3: One group of scientific ideas of key importance in the history of energy has been omitted entirely because of its difficulty. This is the development of thermodynamics in the nineteenth century, which brought the concept of energy itself clearly into focus. Scientists linked heat, light, mechanical energy, electrical energy and the energy of living creatures into a single system and showed clearly that one form of energy could be changed into others, but not destroyed or created. This was of great practical use in designing new machines like the internal combustion engines. It also contributed to the perception that world supplies of energy were not unlimited. With an able pupil or group who were also studying physics it might be useful to follow up these connections.

4: Many pupils will find it difficult to accept the magical or religious thinking of the sources on pages 130–2, to enter into their world filled with inexplicable mysteries and vengeful spirits who needed to be appeased. There is a danger that pupils might look upon the people who held these beliefs as stupid or childish. Exercises 3 and 4 below might be used to tackle this problem.

5: An interesting, important but difficult progression of ideas about machines and why they work bridges the transition between ancient and modern.

Stage 1 The Greeks had gods who were separately responsible for various natural forces like the wind or the sea. For them the explanation of how the water-mill worked in source 36 (page 26) was not, as it seems to us, just a poetic fancy.

Stage 2 Medieval Europeans (pages 134–5), having got rid of water nymphs and gods of the wind were much more inclined to suppose that things moved because they were pushed, as source 261 (page 135) demonstrates on a cosmic scale. God and his angels provided a motive force from the outside. Source 261 also demonstrates that medieval Europeans were familiar with machines. Source 259 page 134 is further evidence of this.

Stage 3 17th/18th Century Europeans (pages 136–7) inheriting both mechanical mindedness and the ability to think of natural phenomena a parts of a mechanism, produced both Newtonian cosmology and the steam engine.

These complex ideas are glanced at in the text.

Exercises 6 and 7 may help to lead some pupils towards them.

C: **Exercises**

General

a) Make a list (or re-use existing agreed list) of the (ten?) most important changes in the history of energy. Against each write the approximate date.
b) Against those which were influenced by religious thinking write 'R'. Against those influenced by scientific thinking write 'S'.
c) Choose one example of each and explain how the influence worked. Support your answer with evidence.
d) 'After. . . (date) science became an important factor in the history of energy.' Choose a date to fill the blank and explain your choice.

2: People today do not worship fire gods or think that fire is sacred. Why then do we have bonfires and 'perpetual' flames like the Olympic flame?

Prehistoric and ancient

3: Read Source 255 page 132.
a) The rules given in this source could have been made up for practical reasons and for religious reasons. Give examples of each and explain your choices.
b) You are an experienced glass-maker explaining the craft to a young one. Explain to him what might happen if the rules are broken.

4: We know that fire is a chemical reaction in which the things we burn combine with oxygen. The Aborigines in source 251 looked on fire in the same way as we look on. . . a person?. . . a pet animal?. . . a bug-eyed monster?
a) Choose (or think of another possibility) and explain your choice.
b) Does the fact they think in a different way from us show that they are stupid?

5: Study the information about the Alexandrian Greeks on page 134. One of their achievements was in geometry. Euclid (c 300 BC) and Archimedes worked out a much more accurate value of 'pi'. How might this have helped in the development of the water-mill?

'Mechanical mindedness'

6: a) By the time of source 261 (page 135) there were water-mills or windmills in most villages in Europe. Can you suggest how the artist may have been influenced by this?
b) Look at the poem in source 36 page 26. The writer's attitude to machines were different from that shown in source 261. Would people who thought like the artist of source 261 be more likely or less likely than those who thought like source 36 to try to invent new machines or new ways or using power? Explain your answer.

Or: 7: Read source 36 (page 26)
a) How did the writer explain the working of the mill?
b) Why did this explanation seem reasonable at the time?

Read source 259 (page 134) and look at source 261 (page 135)

c) How does the writer of source 259 explain the working of the mills?

d) In order to understand Source 261 the people of the Middle Ages had to be familiar with. . . ? What? Explain your answer.

e) The Europeans of the seventeenth century inherited many ideas from those of the Middle Ages. Use your answers to the earlier parts of this question to explain how this helped them to make many new inventions.

Science and the steam engine

8: a) Make a list of the people mentioned on pages 136–7 whose ideas may have influenced Newcomen's work.

b) What evidence is there on these pages of how these ideas were spread at the time?

c) Look at the diagrams (page 138) showing how Newcomen's engine worked. Do you think that he might have though of it without knowing about the work of the others?

d) What evidence would you look for if you were trying to prove conclusively that Newcomen did or did not know about the scientific discoveries of the others?

9: Boulton is asking a banker to lend him £10,000 to finance the development of Watt's engine. The banker is an educated man who knows some science. What arguments would the banker and Boulton use? Write your answer like a play, or in a group decide what the arguments would be and then tape them. If you wish to, include Watt in the discussion.

10: James Watt was able to make his inventions partly because he lived at the right time and place.

a) Explain briefly the main idea that came to Watt as he was walking on Glasgow Green (page 138)

b) What other scientific work had to be done before Watt could think of this?

c) When and by whom was this done?

d) What other factors helped Watt in addition to scientific knowledge?

19th and 20th centuries

11: List A is a list of energy developments of the 19th and 20th centuries. List B is a list of areas of scientific knowledge.

List A	List B
1. Electricity	a. Chemistry
2. Nuclear energy	b. Physics
3. Town gas	c. Biology
4. Oil	d. Metallurgy
5. I.c. engines	e. Geology
6. Natural gas	

a) Place list A in correct chronological order wih the approximte date for each development. Against each item write the letter of the items in list B which helped to cause it.

b) Choose two(?) paired items and explain clearly how the knowledge in list B helped to cause the development in list A.

c) Could the development have happened at all without the scientific knowledge?

d) What other factors besides scientific knowledge helped to cause your chosen developments?

7: Revision and assessment 2

After studying selected factors pupils might be assessed for a second time. An assessment at this stage should be designed to ascertain (1) how far they have in fact consolidated their grasp of the narrative, and (2) whether they have achieved the ojectives of the factors studied.

For the first purpose some of the suggested items from pages 32–3, or variants of them, might be used. For the second, some of the questions suggested above as exercises for each of the factors will be found appropriate, or can be used as a basis for variants.

To construct other questions the following generalised patterns may be of use:

1: At what times and places was the factor an important influence?

2: At what times and places was it of little importance?

3: Did it become significantly more or less important through time or at specific times?

4: Was its effect encourage or to inhibit change, or both?

5: Can it be said that without this factor certain important changes could not possibly have happened?

6: What other factors, if any, had to be present for the chosen factor to have its effect?

8: Teaching the problems

Introduction

A: **Objectives**
After having used this section of the book pupils should be able to:

1: Grasp the story-line of the narrative more fully and recall its details more clearly.

2: (Change and development)

a) Identify periods of rapid and slow change in the history of energy and discuss the reasons for them.

b) Identify trends and turning points in the history of energy and discuss their importance.

c) Identify lines of development and periods of progress or regress in the history of energy as a whole or in parts of it.

3: (Causation)

a) Describe how several causative factors combined together to bring about significant changes.

b) Distinguish between long-term and short-term causative factors.

c) Discuss the role of leading individuals in causing changes in the history of energy.

B: **The structure of this section of the 'guide'**

The Problems section of the book is desinged to be used very much in connection with what has been learned already, pulling 'Energy through Time' together into as much sense in the mind of each pupil as is possible. So much of it consists of charts, pictures and questions intended to lead the reader back into the narrative. The 'guide' does not, therefore, set out systematically to provide a further set of questions, but provides instead a commentary on the materials and on how they may be used.

C: **Teaching strategies**

All of the chapters in the 'problems' section should be studied, since each of them deals with a key idea, but the content chosen to exemplify the ideas is not of itself important. An exception to this is the material on the coming of steam power in 'Why did it Happen Then?' (pages 153–7). The introduction of the steam engines is so central an event in the history of energy that all pupils should study the reasons why it happened.

In many 'problems' chapters several alternative examples of an idea are given. They often vary in difficulty and teachers should select as appropriate. They should also be ready to set alternative examples using the narrative or other materials. It may be useful for pupils, having grasped an idea in the context of 'ready made' materials, to work on further examples for themselves using the index.

Teachers may decide to set individuals or groups of pupils to study some of the 'problem' chapters by themselves. Since each of these chapters is designed with a particular idea in mind, the discussion and the questions do much more to direct the reader than in the rest of the book. They are not, however, designed as work instructions.

The material on progress and regress is placed last because other ideas like trends, development and turning points are components of it. Apart from this the chapters may be taken in any order.

Problems 1: the speed of change
pages 142–5

The main aim of this chapter is to help pupils to identify periods of rapid and of slow change and to see that at times of extensive social and economic change such as the coming of the first civilisation and the coming of industrialisation, technological change was rapid. A teacher might first use the material on page 143, where the contrast is made very clearly, to bring pupils to suggest the importance of differences in the socio-economic background, and then apply this idea to the events in the time chart. The third question on page 142 (Why so few water-mills in Ancient Rome?) could lead pupils to the idea that inventions are of little importance unless the background is ripe for them. The cartoon about Leonardo and the flying machine on page 141 makes the same point.

Pages 144–5 point out that changes can be intermittent or can stop altogether, and that people feeling their way through the maze of unfolding events find it hard to identify these blind alleys of change. Suggestions from pupils of contemporary changes which might turn out to be blind alleys could include the petrol engine, nuclear power or civilisation. It is to be hoped that some pupils will suggest that one way to tell which change is likely to continue is to study history.

Other examples of dead ends or false dawns are steam cars and aeroplanes (page 55) and horse powered locomotives (page 106).

Problems 2: Trends and turning points

This chapter begins by establishing the concept of trend and turning point. Although the words are commonplace it is not likely that pupils will have thought precisely about them. Pupils may then apply these concepts to one or more of four topics, Energy in the Kitchen, Energy to drive machines, human uses of fire, and the development of electricity.

The material about the kitchen on pages 146–8 is probably the easiest to use, and is designed with the weaker readers in mind. The material on electricity on page 151 is the most demanding.

Index entries would enable trends and turning points to be sought in many other areas, for instance use of coal, use of horses, energy for lighting or use of oil. A teacher might decide to set pupils first to study one of the 'ready-made' trends and then to study one based on the use of the index.

1: **Energy in the kitchen**

Some trends:

a) Improvements in methods of baking bread.

b) Improvements in methods of roasting meat.

c) More economical uses of fuel (but note evidence of regress from charcoal to open wood fire in the Bayeux Tapestry).

d) Development of labour saving machinery and devices.

Some turning points:

a) Egypt – first evidence of bread, pots, servants.

b) Introduction of iron in Roman picture

c) Chimney first seen in 18th century picture

d) Introducton in turn of coal, gas, electricity, hot water systems.

Teachers might find it necessary to warn pupils that these pictures are in no way evidence of the earliest date at which a new technique was introduced.

These pictures might be used for purposes unconnected with trends and turning points.
a) (Speed of change) Which features of energy use in the kitchen stayed the same for long periods? When did the most rapid change take place? Why?
b) (Causation) This picture is of a typical kitchen of. . . (time and place). Why did the people of that time and place have kitchens like that?

2: **Energy to drive machines** (page 149)

The massive but rather uneven movement towards more power is the clearest trend. Pupils might also look for trends within the separate type of engine e.g. water-powered engines or steam engines.

Pupils might be asked to look for the largest jumps in the energy used by machines. They could then use their knowledge of the narrative to suggest reasons for these, and to consider whether they should be classed as turning points. Possibles are:

Both steam power and water power increase about 1800 because of the coming of factories.

Steam power increased greatly 1712–1876, because coal provided pre-packaged energy on quite a new scale.

The 20th century growth in the power of steam and water turbines dwarfs all the other changes. It was electrical trnamission of energy that made these vast machines worthwhile.

3: **The uses of fire** (page 150)

The most likely suggestion of a trend is that more and more new ways of using fire have been added with intermittent but increasing frequency.

Pupils might suggest a turning point after 1700 and link it with the energy revolution that began then. More sophisticated suggestions:
a) The steam engine is the first example of the use of fire to produce mechanical energy.
b) The early locomotive shown in the illustration represents the beginning of the use of heat energy for transport.

The trends initiated by both these events are represented by later items in the chart, and pupils may be able to suggest others.

4: **The development of electricity** (page 151)

Pupils might refer back to pages 57–64 to make a case for the work of Volta, Faraday, Gramme, Edison or Tesla to be considered turning points within the period of the time chart. When the question is related to the history of energy as a whole, however they may decide that the Tesla/Westinghouse a.c. system was the real turning point, since it enabled energy in very large amounts to be transmitted widely in home, factory and mine. Reference back to the figures on page 149 should help to confirm this conclusion.

5: **Which changes are important?** (page 152)

This material is self-explanatory. As well helping pupils to think clearly about the idea of historical importance, it forms a useful general revision exercise, and one to which teachers could easily produce variants.

Problems 3: Why did it happen then?
pages 153–7

This chapter and the next deal with problems of cause and motive. In this chapter a case study of the development of the steam engine is used to disentangle the impersonal factors involved. The motives of Boulton and Watt are more fully dealt with in the next chapter on pages 161–5. Some teachers may wish to use the two chapters together, although it is simpler to take them one at a time. In any case a full answer to the central question of this chapter can only be given when individual motives have also been considered in detail. The aim of both chapters is to help pupils to study the web of inter-related factors which are necessary to explain why events happen.

The scientific background of the coming of steam has been dealt with on pages 136–8, and it is assumed that pupils have used this as well as the relevant parts of the narrative.

The main question in this chapter is 'Why did the steam engine develop in 18th century Britain?' It is first split into two components:
1. Why was Newcomen's successful steam pump developed?
2: Why was it developed into the rotative engine by Watt and Boulton?

Suggested strategy

A: **Class discussion**

The reasons for an event within the pupils' own experience is first discussed. It could be their presence at school or some recent event in school or the neighbourhood. Pupils are likely to be able to suggest a set of causes. If these are mainly personal the teacher might move them on to a more general and historical plane by judicious questions. Diagram J shows the sort of ideas which might emerge. A diagram of this sort, built up on the black-board could be as simple or as complex as was appropriate. A few second order causes and causal interrelations are indicated, and some useful general categories into which the causes and motives might be grouped.

B: Separate groups or individuals take each of the questions on page 153, and find answers and supporting evidence about first the Newcomen engine and then the rotative engine. The group dealing with scientific knowledge should refer back to pages 136–8. If personal motives are to be included at this stage, appropriate questions should be set to groups working with pages 161–5. (There is little evidence about Newcomen's motives but see source 261 page 137, as well as page 155)

Figure J

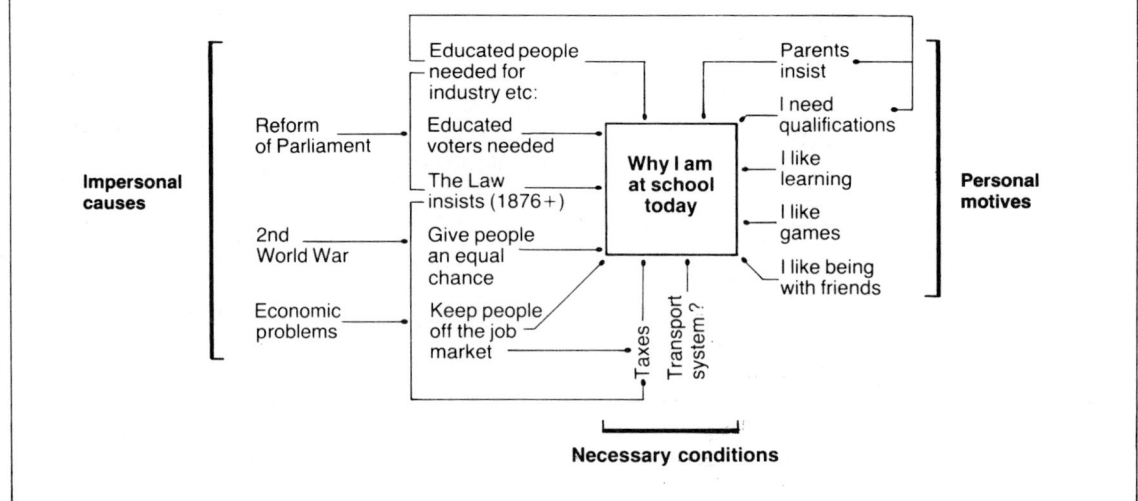

Figure K

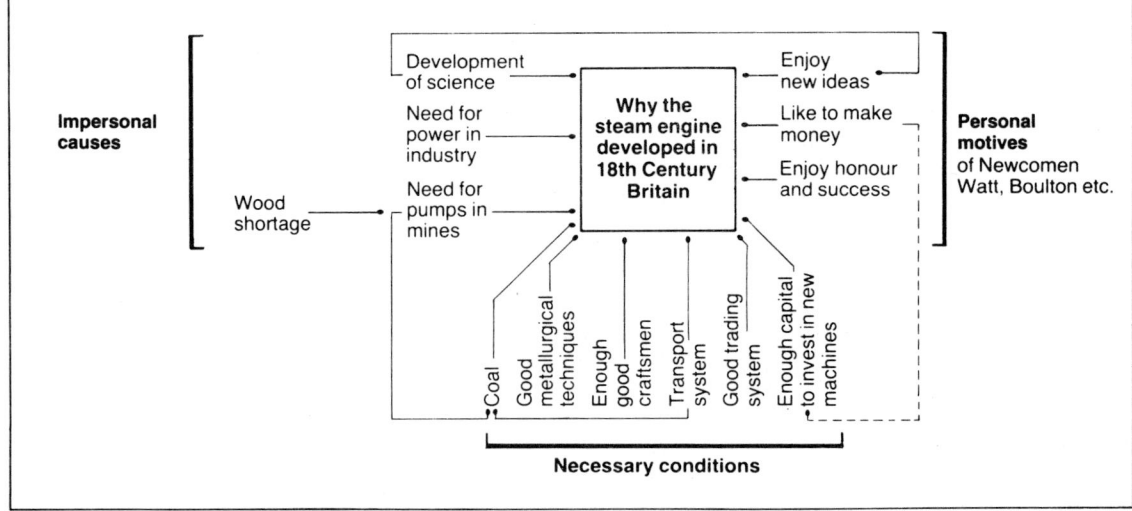

C: Report back, class discussion and compilation of an agreed causation diagram on the lines of diagram K. A diagram of this sort should be a useful revision tool. Its compilation might be done in two stages on the two engines, or all at once. If the personal factors have been left till later it is important that the diagram should have a 'watch this space' component to mark their absence.

9: Discussion of the Hero material on page 157. It should by this time be so overwhelmingly obvious that Hero lacked nearly all the necessary conditions for the coming of steam that 'Why not in Alexandria?' is seen as, historically, a silly question.

E: **Some exercises**

1: If Hero had a speech bubble in the cartoon page 157, what would he be saying? (or what would you add to Hero's thought bubble?) Explain your answer.

2: You are offered a job as the operator of a Savery engine in the year 1702. You need the job badly. Would you accept? Explain your reasons.

3: Thomas Newcomen never wrote an account of making his engine. Write one for him, using source 262 page 137 and any other material you can find.

4: People sometimes say that an idea 'Was ahead of its time'

a) Explain what this might mean giving examples from the history of the steam engine.
b) What other examples from the history of energy can you suggest? (Water-power in Roman times? Motor vehicles in 13th century? Source 260 page 135? Leonardo's helicopter page 141?)

5: Make a 'causation diagram' or write an explanation of why *one* of the following happened where and when it did:

a) Water power
b) Guns and gunpowder
c) The motor car
d) Nuclear power
   (Index entries will help with these and many other possibilities, but a task like this might also lead to useful wider reading.)

This chapter provides material to help pupils to consider the role of individual inventors and pioneers in the history of energy. (Objectives 3 c) and d) on page 37 above) It should enable them to answer questions about the motives of these pioneers and about their importance in bringing about change.

Material is provided on Abraham Darby I, Matthew Boulton and Thomas Edison. The Boulton section provides enough material for the same questions to be answered about James Watt. Pages 161–3, which deal with the motives of Boulton and Watt are essential reading to complete the work on the case study of the steam engine 'Why did it happen then?' (See above pages 38–40 of this 'guide') Apart from this, these three sections on individuals are designed as alternatives, though some pupils may have time to study two or all three of them.

A teacher might decide to set different individuals or groups to work on different people, or to substitute other people of importance in the history of energy on whom books are available in the school library. The narrative would provide background support for work on Newcomen, Faraday, Rockefeller, and Einstein or Rutherford, about whom biographical material is likely to be found, and also on Vitruvius and Tesla on whom it is less likely. Archimedes is the one relevant ancient figure likely to appear in the library catalogue, but his biographical details are so dubious and his links with energy history so arguable that he would not make an effective individual study.

The suggestions that follow are organised under the headings of the three sections of this chapter, but they follow a common pattern and a teacher who wished to set a class to work on several sections at the same time should be able to adapt them quite easily.

Abraham Darby I pages 158–60

A suggested strategy

A: Revision discussion to bring out the importance of the use of coke for the expansion of the iron industry and of the iron industry for the 'second energy revolution'.
B: Reading and discussion of Abiah Darby's letter, source 297 page 160 Evaluation of this as evidence of decisions made sixty years earlier.

C: Work with pages 158–60 to lead pupils to find out how Darby came to make his discovery. Work instructions or other guidance should lead them to:
1. Darby's opportunities to learn about coke.
2. Darby's unique position as an iron-founder interested in castings, and not in pig-iron for refining.
3. The possible role of luck or chance in:
a) there being coking coal near Coalbrookdale
b) the steam cylinders providing at exactly the right time a ready market for castings without

which in turn the development of the steam engine would have been delayed.

D: Some exercises or discussion questions

1: What were Darby's motives in developing his new process?
– *or* Write a letter dated 1711 from Abraham Darby telling a friend in Bristol that he has started to use coke and explaining why.

2: What were the results of his process?

3: Does it seem likely that Darby expected these results to follow?

4: What special factors enable Darby to think of this process, rather than somebody else?

5: What element of luck or chance was there in these events?

6: Would somebody else have developed this process in any case, even if Darby had never lived?

Matthew Boulton (and James Watt) pages 161–4

A suggested strategy

A: Revision discussion of the importance of the steam engine in the history of energy.
B: Discussion of Watt's invention, referring back to page 138 or to work already done relating Watt to the scientific movement of the mid 18th century. Was someone else likely to follow the same chain of reasoning as did Watt once the discoveries of Black became widely known?

This additional source might be used

'He was not so presumptuous as to think that there were not and are not numbers of mechanics in the nation who from the same or even fewer hints would not have completed a better engine than he did.'
James Watt 1794, quoted in A Briggs *'The Power of Steam'* 1982

C: Work with pages 161–4 designed to lead pupils to see.
1. That Boulton's contributions of capital, credit, confidence, skill and vision were of great importance.
2. That luck or chance played a part in bringing Watt together first with the problem of the steam engine (page 138) and later with Boulton.

D: Some exercises or discussion questions

1: What were Watt's motives in making his inventions?

or James Watt is asked in 1765 why he is spending so much time working on his plans for a steam engine. Write his reply.

2: What were Boulton's motives in his work with Watt?

3: What were the results of their work?

4: Does it seem likely (or is there evidence to show) that either Watt or Boulton expected these results to follow?

5: What special qualities of character or background contributed to the success of Boulton (or Watt)

or Choose either Boulton or Watt. The following words could be used to describe one or both of them:

Rich, poor, fearful, courageous, clever, persistent, far-sighted, narrow-minded, hard-working, mean, lucky, ingenious.

Choose (five?) of these words and:
a) Give your reasons for applying each to the person of your choice
b) Explain how these qualities together helped or hindered the development of the steam engine.

6: To what extent was chance or luck a factor in the successful development of Watt's improved steam engines?

7: Look again at your work on why the steam engine developed in 18th century Britain.
a) How important was the contribution of Boulton (or Watt or both) compared with the impersonal factors which helped to bring it about?
b) Would it have developed in Britain in any case even if Watt and Boulton had never lived?

Thomas A Edison pages 165–7

A suggested strategy

A: Revision discussion of the importance of electric light in the coming into use of electricity and of electricity in the history of energy.

B: Reading and discussion of source 312 page 167 – Would electric light qualify as one of 'The incredible changes which he wrought in our civilisation'? Evaluation of the source.

C: Work with pages 58–9 (or revision of work already done) to decide why electric lighting made a sudden advance in the 1880's. Pupils might be able to suggest that simultaneous inventions imply that common (impersonal?) factors may be at work.

D: Work with pages 165–7 to lead pupils to find out:
1. Edison's motives.
2. That his contribution to the coming of electric light was in the organisation of research and in marketing, rather than in invention.
3. The possible role of luck or chance in Edison coming to combine the right experience in electricity, the necessary capital and valuable financial and business contacts just at the time when the Gramme generator was invented (1871).

E: Some exercises
1: Write and/or draw an advertisement to get people to buy shares in a company which Edison is just setting up to make electric lighting equipment in 1879.

2: What were Edison's motives? How successful was he in carrying them out?

3: Look at the two photographs of Edison on page 165 and 167.
a) What sort of person would you think he was from this evidence.
b) Both these photographs are carefully posed. Why should he adopt these poses?
c) Does this evidence fit in with other evidence about his character?
d) Does his character help to explain his career?

4: What contribution did Edison make to the coming of electricity? Would it have happened at much the same time and place if he had never lived?

Problems 5: Progress
pages 168–170

This final chapter provides material to help pupils to refine their use of the terms 'progress' and 'regress' (Objective 2c) on page 37), and also to consolidate their overview of the history of energy through time. As well as forming a natural conclusion to the study in development it also begins a revision process for the final assessment.

There is a fundamental difficulty which arises from the technological nature of the topic. Technological development tends to have a once-for-all character – techniques are difficult or impossible to un-invent. Thus it is easy to set out a series of more and more powerful engines or more and more effective labour-saving devices in a progressive order, but it is hard to find examples of technological regress. For instance in the European Dark Ages people did not forget how to do sophisticated ironwork or how to make water-mills or harness oxen. It is in the effects of technological change, or in social, economic and political change that examples of regress are to be sought.

Page 168 is designed to lead to discussion of this difficulty. The material on sculpture suggests that the area of the arts is different from that of technology, in that it is one to which the idea of improvement or deterioration over time is not appropriate. The last paragraph leads pupils to consider the *results* of technological changes. They should have little difficulty in suggested improved machines that have had harmful effects or cause new difficulties.

Page 169 is also designed as discussion stimulus. (See Exercise A below for a revision exercise based on this page.) Pupils at this stage should find it easy to suggest examples to fit all the suggested patterns. The more thoughtful, who consider the page as a whole will be more puzzled – 'We can find examples to fit all the patterns, but they seem to contradict each other. How can they all be valid?' The difficulty arises basically because words like progress and regress conceal value judgements – they imply a 'worse' and a 'better' that are really matters of opinion and perspective.

Page 170 concentrates attention on this point. Perhaps after using it pupils might be brought to see that the historians' questions are:– 'better in what respects? progress towards what goals? Improvement or deterioration for whom? Progress or regress over what time scale?' (See exercise 2 below)

If historians can offer anything in response to questions like the question of progress, it is in their ability to look at events from various standpoints, as parts of various patterns of change, and in various chronological perspectives.

These are deep waters for pupils and for teachers and it is no part of a course for 15–16 year-olds to plumb their depths. But a study in development should take note of their existence and warn its users that careful navigation is needed to sail them without shipwreck.

Exercises

1: Look at the drawings on page 169 illustrating various ideas about progress and regress.

a) Write down a title for each idea.
b) Against each of your titles write (three?) examples from the history of energy, giving the approximate date of each or the date when it began and when it ended.
c) Choose *one* of your examples and justify your choice.

2: What arguments can be put for and against (one of?) the following as examples of progress.

a) The taming of horses by early nomadic tribes c. 2000 BC

b) The development of extensive slavery in the early civilisations
c) The introduction of the windmill into a medieval village
d) Increased iron production in Europe 1300–1600
e) The development of the internal combustion engine in the nineteenth century.

Before you write your answer think of:

a) The different points of view of different people affected by the change. (e.g. rich and poor)
b) The different areas of life which the change influenced differently (e.g. it may have had a different influence on warlike and on peaceful activities)
c) The different effects of the change over long and over short time-spans (e.g. on people living at the time and on people 100 years later)
d) How the change fits into different trends (e.g. a trend to cut down human labour or a trend to use up fossil fuels)

3: Choose one of the following statements with which you agree or disagree. Explain your reasons:

a) The coming of nuclear power is progress, so you can't stop it.
b) History tells a story of man's increasing pollution of the earth and destruction of its resources, so things will have to change soon.
c) People who have to make decisions about energy policy should know about the history of energy through time.

9: Revision and assessment 3

Revision

Exercises such as those suggested on pages 30–1 and 39 of this guide for the revision of the narrative and of the factors studied will also be useful for final revision. As far as the study of problems in the final part of the work is concerned, this is itself a revision activity covering the whole syllabus.

Trial paper

The remaining need is to familiarise pupils with the style of examination questions and papers. For this teachers will rely mainly on the past papers or sample papers of the examination board of their choice. All the boards, however base their papers on a syllabus differing little from the 'Target Objectives' set out on page 3 above, and all are concerned to set papers which will measure the attainment of these objectives and will not instead measure the mastery of a mass of learned detail or of predigested answers to stock questions.

The following sample paper and marking scheme were drafted by the Project in 1985. They are designed to be accessible to the whole of the GCSE range of ability. They follow the regulations and style of the Southern Examination Group's Joint Examination on the Project syllabus, and teachers using examination boards outside this group should take them as general guidance only.

Study in development

Sample paper

Energy through Time

This was Part I of a two hour paper, Part II being the Depth Study.
Candidates were advised to spend 1 hour and 20 minutes on Part I.

Answer all parts of Questions 1 and 2 and *either* Questions 3A *or* Question 3B

Question 1

Study the following sources carefully.

SOURCE A
Carving of a horse driven mill.
Rome.

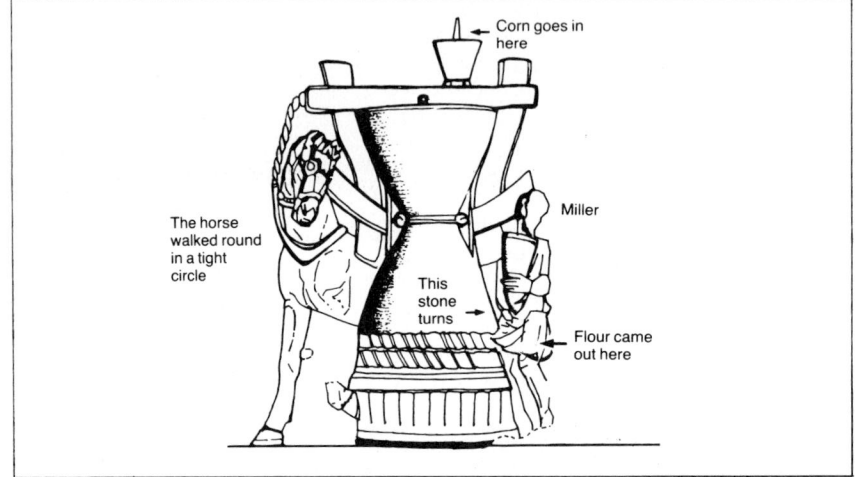

SOURCE B
Hydro electric power station,
Brazil.

SOURCE C
Drawing of a water mill from a
German manuscript.

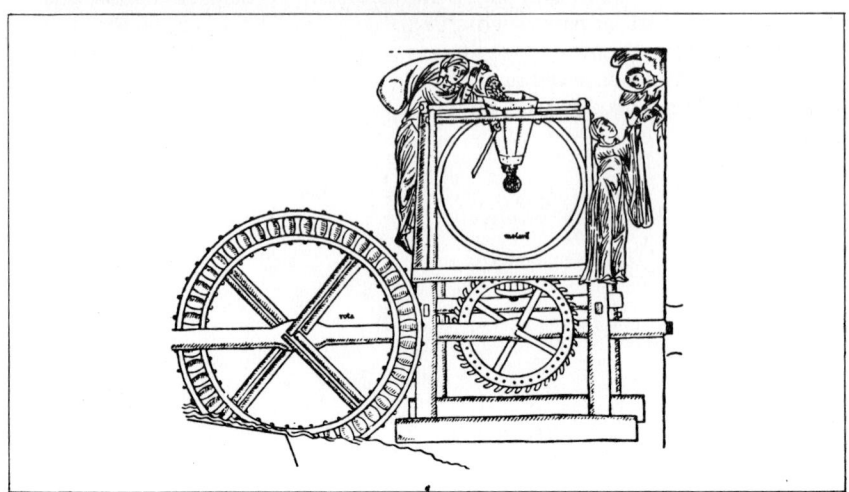

SOURCE D
Model of woman grinding corn
with a hand mill, Egypt.

Now answer the following questions.

(a) Write down the letter of the sources A to D in the order in which the developments they refer to happened.

2 marks

(b) Could these developments have happened in any other order, or is this most unlikely? Explain your answer.

8 marks

(c) Three of these developments A, B and C increased man's control of energy. Which *one* of them was the biggest step forward? Explain your answer.

10 marks

Total 20 marks

Question 2   Study the following sources carefully.

SOURCE E

'*Stop your grinding, you women who toil at the mill. Sleep late, even though the cocks crow to tell you it is dawn. The corn goddess has ordered the water nymphs to do the work your arms used to do. They leap down on top of the wheel and turn the axle with its revolving spokes. Then it turns the heavy mill-stones.*'
Greek poem 1st century BC.

SOURCE F
Modern diagram showing the
working of a jet aero engine.

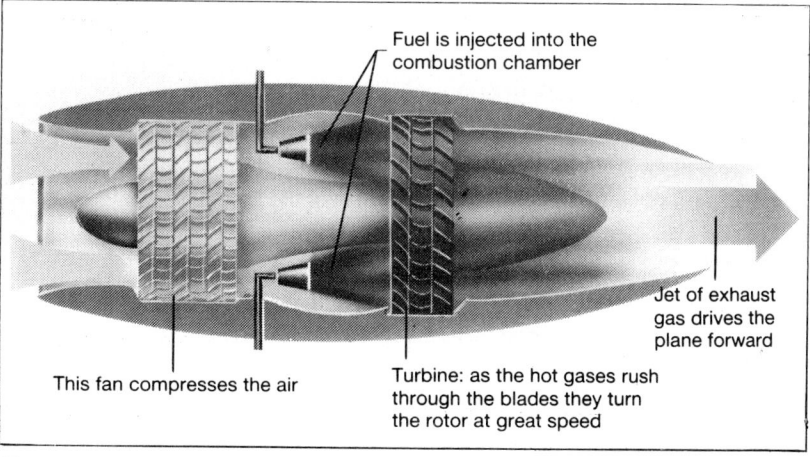

Now answer the following questions.

(a) The writer of Source E describes an early water mill. By what source of power did he think it was driven?

1 mark

(b) Why did the explanation in Source E seem sensible to people in the first century BC?

9 marks

(c) The machine in Source F is driven by the hot gases made by burning fuel. Why would the people of the first century BC find it impossible to understand the modern explanation given in Source F?

10 marks

Now study Source G.

SOURCE G
Painting made in France in the 14th century AD. It shows angels turning handles which keep the sky and the stars moving round.

Now answer the following.

(d) In what way does Source G show that people in the 14th century AD were still thinking as they did in the 1st century BC?

3 marks

(e) In what way does it show that they were thinking like modern people?

7 marks

(f) Source E is written by a poet, using his imagination. Does this mean that his explanation is of no use to the historian?

10 marks

Total 40 marks

Question 3

Answer *either* Questions 3A *or* Question 3B.

Either
Question 3A

In the History of Energy people have sometimes opposed the coming of a new technique or the continuation of an old one. Choose *one* technique that was opposed. (You may wish to choose one of: slavery; use of coal; power-driven machines in factories; alternating current electricity, but you may choose another development if you wish).

(a) Say briefly what the development was.

2 marks

(b) Say what sorts of people opposed it and explain their reasons for doing so.

8 marks

(c) 'People who oppose change stand in the way of progress.' Do you agree? Support your answer with examples from any part of the history of energy.

10 marks

Total 20 marks

or
Question 3B.

Do not answer this question if you have answered Question 3A.

The steam engine was developed by Newcomen, Watt and others in Britain in the 18th century.

(a) How did developments in mining help to cause this?

2 marks

(b) What other factors also helped. Explain how.

8 marks

(c) What was the importance of the steam engine in the History of Energy?

10 marks

Total 20 marks

10: Energy through Time

Sample marking scheme

Introduction

In general marks are not awarded for specific correct information, although there are exceptions such as Question 2(a). This does not mean that the need for precise and accurate facts is to be undervalued. But this mark scheme is designed to give no credit for irrelevant information, however accurate. The conceptual level of the answer gives access to a band of marks, and *within that band* the answer which is well supported by relevant and accurate facts should be given the higher marks.

If, in an examiner's view, a candidate *must necessarily* have operated at a given conceptual level to have written what he did, then the answer should be marked at that level even though the concept is not explicitly spelled out by the candidate. Marks are to be given for the level of historical thinking and understanding rather than for clarity of expression.

Question 1		**20 marks**	
	(a)	2 marks for correct order D, A, C, B. Deduct one mark for each misplaced item.	2 marks
Level 1:	(b)	8 marks Mere assertion that no variation possible, or very vague and woolly 'a priori' argument based on a naive assumption that progressive development is inevitable.	1 mark
Level 2:		Logical but not historical. e.g. handmill simplest so earliest, or power station most complex so latest.	
		Top of band for answers dealing effectively with all four.	2–4 marks
Level 3:	(i)	Argument based on the idea that the distinctive use of slave/animal power in ancient times, water power in the Middle Ages, and complex high technology energy in modern times, possible only in the appropriate historical context.	
	(ii)	Well-developed arguments that the order could be different. e.g. regress possible, or technologies overlap extensively chronologically.	
	(iii)	*Well argued* answers based on the cumulative nature of technological development.	5–8 marks
	(c)	10 marks	
Level 1:		Naive view-most power most important, so B.	5–8 marks
Level 2:		Interpret 'step forward' in relation to short-term results of chosen development e.g. hydro station transmits energy to many distant cities, factories etc., so B. Little historical discussion.	2–4 marks
Level 3:		Historical argument e.g. water power was the first mechanical power and made possible later changes such as Industrial Revolution in 18th century or modern water turbines in power stations.	5–10 marks
			Total 20 marks

Question 2		**40 marks**	
	(a)	'Nymphs', or Water. He only made up the nymphs.'	1 mark
	(b)	9 marks	
Level 1:		Unhistorical explanations which assume that people then were stupid or ignorant.	1 mark
Level 2:		Explanations which recognise that people then had different *knowledge*. e.g. were unfamiliar with mechanical power.	2–4 marks
Level 3:		Explanations which recognise that people then had a different *perspective* e.g. found it natural to assume that things not moved by muscles were moved by magic.	6–9 marks
	(c)	**10 marks**	
Level 1:		As in (b) Level 1 above.	1 mark
Level 2:		Uses details of Source F, and explains that people of 100 BC quite unfamiliar with each of these.	2–6 marks
Level 3:		Explanations based on the understanding that the whole scientific and technological world of Source F is alien to the minds of people of earlier periods.	6–10 marks

	(d)	3 marks	
Level 1:		Describes the working of Source G but no comparison.	1 mark
Level 2:		Motive power supernatural in both cases.	2–3 marks

(e) 7 marks (difficult questions so be generous). Anything getting anywhere near the idea that G assumes that people are familiar with machines, because it uses a mechanical analogy to explain the universe.

(f) 10 marks

Level 1:	Accepts the suggestion but does not really discuss it.	1 mark
Level 2:	Accepts, but supports this with sensible argument e.g. that history is based on precise evidence about the real world, unlike Source E.	1–3 marks
Level 3:	Rejects on the grounds that poems etc. can be used as evidence e.g. that water-mills did exist at that time.	3–5 marks
Level 4:	Rejects on the grounds that the historian's task is to understand the ideas and attitudes of people of the past, including the contents of their imaginations.	5–10 marks

Total 40 marks

Question 3A 20 marks

(a) 2 marks – one mark per precise point in brief explanation.

(b) 8 marks

(a) 'Sorts of people' – 2 marks.
One mark per sort e.g. hand-loom weavers opposed power machines.

(b) Reasons for opposition–6 marks.

Level 1:	Explanation historically valid, but narrowly practical. e.g. factory discipline was harsh and unpleasant.	1–3 marks
Level 2:	Explanation develops the special perspective of the opponents. (e.g. people in the domestic system worked irregular hours, were used to natural rythmn and found the steady grind of machines unpleasant)	4–6 marks

(c) 10 marks

Level 1:		Naive acceptance with no valid e.g.'s.	1 mark
Level 2:		Accepts giving reasonable and effective e.g.'s.	2–5 marks
Level 3:	(a)	Argues, with examples that change is not necessarily progressive.	
	(b)	Argues, with examples that opposition can force the refining and improvements of a new idea.	6–10 marks

Total 20 marks

Question 3B 20 marks

(a) One mark per precise point in brief explanation 2 marks.

(b) 8 marks.

Level 1:	Able to choose a valid factor, but no worthwhile explanation e.g. Plenty of coal in Great Britain. Development of iron working. Scientific advances. Need for power in factories. Availability of capital. 1 mark per choice (max 4)	4 marks
Level 2:	Makes choice as Level 1 but explain how chosen factor(s) led to steam engine. 2 marks per choice (max 8) if gives many factors. Full 8 marks for	

candidates who deal with only two or three factors, but show how they were inter-related. 4–8 marks

(c) 10 marks **Maximum marks**

Level 1: Vague and naive answers e.g. 'It gave a lot more power.' 1 mark

Level 2: Explains results of coming of steam in 18th/19th century Britain, but with no wider historical perspective. 2–5 marks

Level 3: Long-term historical importance assessed e.g. made possible the 'high energy' society, by enabling the production of mechanical power from fossil fuels, unlike energy technologies available before then. 5–10 marks

Total 20 marks

11: Additional resources

Places to visit

Health Warning. Many of the museums listed below prepare work materials but neither these nor the organisation of the exhibits themselves are likely to be related to the 'Energy through Time' course. It is almost essential for a teacher to make an advance visit to plan the work. A well-prepared visit to a small local site can be far more useful then the indigestible surfeit which a badly planned major visit can become.

Alternative energy and conservation

The Centre for Alternative Technology, Machynlleth, Powys, Wales. Write (send s.a.e.) to the Education Officer.

Telephone 0654–2400

The Urban Centre for Appropriate Technology, 82, Colston Street Bristol, BS1 5BB. Write to the Education Service.

Telephone 0272–662008

Electricity

Power stations. Write to 'Understanding Electricity' at your regional office of the Central Electricity Generating Board.

The Wedgewood Electrical Collection. Christchurch, Dorset. Write to the Curator, Southern Electrical Collection, 25 Bourne Valley Road, Branksome, Poole, Dorset, BH12 1HH.

SE Electricity Board's Museum. Write to The Curator, The Milne Museum, The Slade, Tonbridge, Kent. TN9 1HR

Gas

The East Midlands Gas Museum, Aylestone Road, Leicester. LE2 7QH. Write to the Curator.

Telephone 0533–549414 extension 2192

Mills and early steam engines

There are examples in many parts of the country. See publications on local industrial archaeology.

Nuclear energy

The Sellafield Exhibition, British Nuclear Fuels Ltd, Sellafield Site, Seascale, Cumbria. Write to the Manager, The Exhibition Centre.

Visitors are also welcome at the Atomic Energy Authority's establishment at: Risley, Cheshire; Preston, Lancashire; Windscale, Cumbria; Dounreay, Caithness (Exhibition in summer); Harwell, Oxfordshire; Winfrith, Dorset. Addresses in UKAEA's 'Resources for Teachers' see under 'Sources of information' below.

Coal and Iron

The Abbeydale Industrial Village, Abbeydale Road South, Sheffield. S7 2QW. Write to the Secretary.

Telephone 0742–367731

The Chatterley Whitfield Mining Museum, Chatterley Whitfield Colliery, Tunstall, Stoke-on-Trent. ST6 8UN. Write to the Curator.

Telephone 0782–813337

The Ironbridge Gorge Museum, 3, The Wharfage, Ironbridge, Telford. Write to the Education Officer.

Telephone 0952–3522

General

Beamish Open Air Museum, Stanley, County Durham. DH9 0RG. Write to the Keeper.

Telephone 0207–231811

The Greater Manchester Museum of Science and Industry, Liverpool Road, Manchester 3. Write to the Education Service.

Telephone 061–833–0027

The Science Museum. Write to the Education Service, The Science Museum, Exhibition Road, London SW7 2DD.

Telephone 01–589–3456

Many other museums have exhibits, such as domestic interiors, which can be used as evidence for work on changing energy use.

Sources of information and support materials

The great bulk of the material and information available is concerned with present-day technology or its attendant problems, and is produced with objectives in mind quite different from those of teachers of a study in development. So only a proportion of the material on offer is likely to be useful.

BP Education Service, PO Box 5, Wetherby, West Yorkshire. LS23 7EH

Catalogue free. Most material not free, but much available on free loan from 70 Teachers Centres in all parts of the country. Resource packs on World Energy statistics, Alternative Energy.

BP Film Library, 15, Beaconsfield Road, London NW10 2LE

Free catalogue. Films on free loan.

British Gas Education Service, PO Box 46, Hounslow Middlesex, London TW4 6NF

Catalogue free.

British Gas Film and Video Library, Park Hall Trading Estate, London SE21 8EL.

Catalogue free

British Nuclear Fuels Limited. Film Librarian, Information Services Directorate, BNFL, Risley, Warrington, Cheshire, WA3 6AS.

List free. Free loan of films.

The Central Electricity Generating Board, see Understanding Electricity, (below)

CEGB Film and Video Library, Viscom Limited, Park Hall Road, Trading Estate, London SE21 8EL

List free. Free loan service.

The Centre for Alternative Technology, Machynlleth, Powys, Wales. Information sheets, slide sets etc.

Send s.a.e. to the Education Officer for list.

Department of Energy Information Division, Room 1312, Thames House South, Millbank, London SW1P 4QJ.

Free catalogue. Some free material including 'Energy a Key Resource', booklet 20 pages and 'UK Energy Statistics' (annual)

Friends of the Earth, 377 City Road, London EC1V 1NA

Send s.a.e. for list. Leaflets, briefing papers etc. Emphasis on renewables and pollution.

National Coal Board Schools Service, Room 351, Hobart House, London SW1X 7AE.	Free pupil booklet. Some support materials for projects on coal.
The Shell Film Library, 25 The Burroughs, Hendon, London NW4 4AT.	Catalogue free. Film and video on free loan.
Understanding Electricity Education Service, 30 Millbank, London SW1P 4RD	Free talks service. Catalogue Free. Wallcharts, Film, Video filmstrips, booklets. Free or free loan. 'Centenary of Service' useful 98 page booklet on development of electricity. Free. 16 page booklet 'Power from the Wind', Set of Wallcharts Electricity Through Ages.'
The United Kingdom Atomic Energy Authority, Information Service Branch, 11 Charles II Street, London SW1Y 4QP.	Free catalogue of resources for teachers. Teaching pack, pamphlets, booklets, audio visual material. Talks service.

Audio-visual aids		
	Acid Rain. 35 minute colour film o video. Viscom Limited, Park Hall Road. Trading Estate, London SE21 8EL.	Free.
	Discovering Electricity. 40 minute colour film on history of electricity. Understanding Electricity Film Service, 15, Beaconsfield Road, London NW10 2LE.	Free.
	The Energy Problem. The Nuclear Solution. 15 minute colour film. Nuclear power Information Group. Viscom Limited, Park Hall Road, Trading Estate, London SE21 8EL.	Free.
	Energy within reason. 21 minute colour film discussing alternative to oil. BP Film Library, 15, Beaconsfield Road, London NW10 2LE.	
	Eye on the Future. 23 minute colour film or video. Alternatives to oil. The Shell Film Library, 25, The Burroughs, Hendon, London NW4 4AT.	Free
	A History of the Oil Engine, 1861–1901 Black and white film. The Shell film Library, 25, The Burroughs, Hendon, London NW4 4AT.	Free
	A History of Windmills. Slides and cassette. Longmans. Serial number 35660.	Free.
	The Magic Metal (Uranium) 15 minute colour film or video. UKAEA Viscom Limited, Park Hall Road, Trading Estate, London SE21 8EL	
	Power from the Atom. 25 minute colour film or video. UKAEA. History and development of nuclear power. Viscom Limited, Park Hall Road, Trading Estate, London SE21 8EL.	Free.
	Power to the People. 26 minute colour film or video, Development of the national Grid since 1935. Viscom Limited, Park Hall Road, Trading Estate, London SE21 8EL.	Free.
	Renewable energy for today and tommorrow. 60 slides with notes. Centre for Alternative Technology, Machynlleth, Powys, Wales.	
	There will be gas. 18 minute colour film. History of the gas industry. British Gas Film and Video Library, Park Hall Trading Estate, London SE21 8EL.	Free.
	Time for Energy. 33 minute colour film or video. Renewable energy and conservation. The Shell Film Library, 25, The Burroughs, Hendon, London NW4 4AT.	Free.

| | *Your Generation.* 30 minute video. Development of electricity since Faraday. Viscom Ltd, Park Hall Road, Trading Estate, London SE21 8EL. | Free |

Books for teachers

There is no convenient book which covers the whole course. Teachers might find a useful sense of perspective in an overview history such as JM Roberts *'History of the World'* (Hutchinson 1976). For a shorter time-span the Braudel chapter (Middle Ages to c 1800) is magisterial and stimulating. The March 1983 'History Today' provides a useful and not very technical introduction to machines like water-mills with which teachers may not be familiar. Derry and Williams is likely to be the most convenient general reference for most developments before 1900. Sampson provides a convenient summary of the development of the oil industry and a lively discussion of the relationships of the oil companies down to the late 1970s. Chapman or Wild might be used as introduction to today's energy problems and those of the future.

Anon.	*Electricity Supply in the UK (A Chronology 1764–1981)*	Electricity Council, 1982. Free
WHG Armytage	*A Social History of Engineering*	Faber, 1976
F Braudel	*Civilisation and Capitalism* Volume 1 chapter 5	Collins, 1981
D Birdsall and C Cipolla	*The Technology of Man*	Wildwood, 1980
A Briggs	*The Power of Steam*	Michael Joseph, 1982
AF Burstall	*Simple Working Models of Historic Machines*	Edward Arnold, 1968
A Byers	*Centenary of Service*	Electricity Council, 1981. Free
P Chapman	*Fuel's Paradise*	Pelican, 1975
JG Crowther	*A Short History of Science*	Methuen, 1969
MA Daumas	*A History of Technology and Invention*	Murray, 1969
TK Derry and TI Williams	*A Short History of Technology from the Earliest Times to AD 1900*	Oxford University Press, 1960
G Foley	*The Energy Question*	Pelican, 1976
RAS Hennessey	*The Electrical Revolution*	Oriel, 1972
Various authors	*History Today* March 1983. Articles on Muscle Power, water power, wind power, power from the sea.	
TP Hughes	*Thomas Edison*	HMSO [Science Museum], 1976
DS Landes	*The Unbound Prometheus*	Cambridge University Press, 1969
E Larsen	*A History of Invention.* Especially first section on energy inventions.	Dent, 1961
L. Lyson	*British Water Mills*	Batsford, 1964
JK Major	*Animal Powered Engines*	Batsford, 1978
J Needham	Articles on Chinese Science and Technology in *The Legacy of China*	Oxford University Press, 1964
P Odell	*Oil and world power*	Penguin, 1983
A Raistrick	*Dynasty of Ironfounders* About the Darby family	David and Charles, 1970
LTC Rolt	*James Watt*	Batsford, 1962
A Sampson	*The Seven Sisters* About the oil multinationals	Hodder and Stoughton, 1980
JD Storer	*A Simple History of the Steam Engine*	John Baker, 1969
S Strandh	*Machines, an Illustrated History*	Beazley, 1979
L Syson	*British water Mills*	Batsford, 1964
AR Ubberlohde	*Man and Energy*	Pelican, 1963
RA Wailes	*Source Book of Windmills and Water-mills*	Ward Lock, 1979

L White	*Medieval Technology and Social Change*	Oxford University Press, 1962
M Wild	*Energy in the 80s*	Longman, 1980
David Wilson	*Rutherford – Simple Genius*	Hodder and Stoughton
M Wilson (Ed)	*Energy*	Time-Life, 1963
D Yarwood	*The British Kitchen*	Batsford, 1981

Books for pupils

It is not suggested that any class-book apart from *Energy through Time* is necessary. The following books may be useful for individual study of particular problems. Many of the books listed above are also quite accessible to most pupils and many of those below will be useful to teachers.

O Ashmore	*The Development of Power in Britain*	Macmillan, 1967
I Asimov	*How we found out about Nuclear Power*	Longman, 1982
E Catherall	*Water Power*	Wayland, 1981
JG Crowther	*Six Great Engineers* They include Westinghouse, Parsons and Diesel	Hamish Hamilton, 1959
F Frazer	*Discovering Energy*	Longman, 1982
B Gunston	*Coal*	Watts, 1981. A title in the 'Energy' series
	Faraday and Electricity. Jackdaw Publications, Number 86	Jonathan Cape
	James Watt and Steam-Power. Jackdaw Publications, Number 13	Johnathan Cape
E Larsen	*Men who Changed the World* They include Edison, Parsons and Rutherford.	Phoenix, 1952
BR Lewis	*Steam Engines* A title in the 'Eyewitness Histories' series	Wayland, 1978
A MacGregor	*Windmills* A project series for young people	Evans, 1982
JF Moon	*Rudolf Diesel and the Diesel Engine*	Wayland, 1982
A Nahum	*James Watt and the Power of Steam*	Wayland, 1981
SN Payne	*Wind and Water Energy*	Blackwell
LTC Rolt	*Great Engineers* They include Darby and Newcomen	Bell, 1962
J Ross	*Thomas Edison*	Hamilton, 1982
H Thompson	*Engineers and Engineering*	Batsford, 1976
JNT Vince	*Windmills*	Blackwell, 1975
H Weiss	*Motors and Engines and how they work* It includes simple models to make	Hamish Hamilton, 1969
N Wynne	*Inventions*	Hamlyn, 1981

Books and articles about the Schools History Project

Books

	Project, *A New Look at History*	Holmes McDougall, 1976
DJ Shemilt	*History 13–16 Evaluation Study*	Holmes McDougall, 1980
DJ Shemilt	*'Beauty and the Philosopher: Empathy in History and Classroom'* in AK Dickinson (Ed), *Learning History*	Heinemann, 1984
Project Team and SREB	Explorations in Teaching SCHP History	Southern Regional Examinations Board, 1984

Booklets

Available from the Director at Trinity and All Saints College, Horsforth, Leeds. LS18 5HD

1. Course Structure and Materials
2. Teaching Approaches
3. Introduction to Coursework

Articles

F Blow	'History and Computers' *Teaching History*, 33	June 1982
AJ Boddington	'Empathy and the Teaching of History' *British Journal of Educational Studies* Volume xxvii no. 1	February 1980
AJ Boddington	'Schools Council Project: History 13 – 16,' *History Teaching Review*	October 1976
I Dawson	'What shall we do with the Third Year?' *Teaching History*, 29	February 1981
V Kelly	History Around Us: The Experience of four Belfast schools, *Teaching History*, 34	October 1980
HG Macintosh	'Schools Council Project History 13 – 16: The CSE Examination, some problems of assessment', *Teaching History*, 24 and 25	June/October 1979
J Scott	'Content and Concepts', *Teaching History*, 31	October 1981
DJ Shemilt	'Historical Understanding at Upper Secondary Level', *Trends in Education,*	Spring 1978
DJ Shemilt	'Schools Council Project History 13 – 16: Past, Present and Future', *History Teaching Review*	April 1980
DJ Shemilt	'The Devil's Locomotive,' *History and Theory*	1983
J Wilmut and AJ Boddington	'The Development of a Common 16+ Examination for SCHP 13 – 16,' *Teaching History*, 40	October 1984